Peter,
Stephen,
James,
and John

STUDIES IN EARLY NON-PAULINE CHRISTIANITY

Peter, Stephen, James, and John

STUDIES IN EARLY NON-PAULINE CHRISTIANITY

by

F. F. BRUCE

Grand Rapids
WILLIAM B. EERDMANS PUBLISHING COMPANY

© 1979 F. F. Bruce

First published 1979 by the Paternoster Press, England,
under the title *Men and Movements in the Primitive Church*

First American edition published 1980
through special arrangement with Paternoster by
Wm. B. Eerdmans Publishing Co.
255 Jefferson Ave. S.E.
Grand Rapids, Michigan 49503

First paperback edition 1994

Printed in the United States of America

Library of Congress Cataloging-in-Publication Data

Bruce, Frederick Fyvie, 1910-1990.
Peter, Stephen, James, and John.
Includes index.
1. Church history — Primitive and early church,
ca. 30-600 — Addresses, essays, lectures.
I. Title.
BR165.B7145   1980   270.1   80-11501
ISBN 0-8028-0849-2

To
Frederick William Ratcliffe

CONTENTS

ABBREVIATIONS

ACO	*Acta Conciliorum Oecumenicorum* (Berlin/Leipzig)
Ant.	*Antiquities* (Josephus)
AV	Authorized (King James) Version (1611)
BJ	*Jewish War* (Josephus)
BJRL	*Bulletin of the John Rylands (University) Library*
BZNW	*Beiheft zur Zeitschrift für die neutestamentliche Wissenschaft*
CD	Book of the Covenant of Damascus
CSEL	*Corpus Scriptorum Ecclesiasticorum Latinorum* (Vienna)
EQ	*Evangelical Quarterly*
E.T.	English Translation
GCS	*Griechische Christliche Schriftsteller* (Berlin)
Hist. Eccl.	*Ecclesiastical History* (Eusebius)
HTR	*Harvard Theological Review*
JBL	*Journal of Biblical Literature*
JTS	*Journal of Theological Studies*
Nat. Hist.	*Natural History* (Pliny)
NEB	New English Bible (1970)
NIV	New International Version (1978)
NTS	*New Testament Studies*
PL	*Patrologia Latina* (Migne)
1QM	War *(Milḥamah)* Scroll from Qumran Cave 1

1QS	Rule (*Serek*) of the Community from Qumran Cave 1
4QFlor	*Florilegium* (Anthology) from Qumran Cave 4
RSV	Revised Standard Version (1952)
RV	Revised Version (1881–85)
TB	Babylonian Talmud
ZNW	*Zeitschrift für die neutestamentliche Wissenschaft*
ZTK	*Zeitschrift für Theologie und Kirche*

PREFACE

The four studies contained in the following pages were presented in March 1979 as the inaugural series of annual Didsbury Lectures in the British Isles Nazarene College, Manchester.

The first three lectures were delivered in an earlier form in the Faculty of Theology, University College, Cardiff, in November 1978. The fourth is the revision of a lecture delivered in the John Rylands University Library, Manchester, in October 1977, under the title "St. John at Ephesus", and published in the Library's *Bulletin* for Spring 1978 (Vol. 60, pp. 339–361); it is reproduced here by kind permission.

My thanks are due to my colleagues and friends in Cardiff and Manchester for giving me the opportunity to deliver these lectures and for many kindnesses shown to me while they were being delivered. My thanks are due also to my friends at The Paternoster Press for their ready willingness to publish them in this form.

September 1979   F.F.B.

INTRODUCTION

When, in May 1959, I was invited to meet the
Committee charged with recommending an appoint-
ment to the Rylands Chair of Biblical Criticism and
Exegesis in the University of Manchester, the late
Professor S. G. F. Brandon (then Dean of the Faculty
of Theology) asked me in what area or areas of
biblical study I hoped to prosecute further research.
I mentioned the history of non-Pauline Christianity
in the first century as one area that attracted me –
possibly because I had then begun work on a
commentary on the Epistle to the Hebrews. I did
keep my promise to the extent of completing that
commentary and also subsequently writing a short
commentary on the Epistles of John. But over the
intervening twenty years I have found myself paying
more and more attention to Pauline studies – in
which indeed I am still deeply involved. Nevertheless, the study of Pauline Christianity demands that
attention be paid to contemporary non-Pauline
Christianity. It is plain from Paul's own writings that
other presentations of the Christian message than
his own were current during his apostolic career.

With some of these other presentations he was quite happy; against others he found it necessary to put his readers on their guard.

The writings of Paul are our earliest datable Christian documents. As such they supply our earliest source-material for non-Pauline as well as for Pauline Christianity. If that means that we have to view important phases of non-Pauline Christianity and its leaders through Paul's eyes, it cannot be helped; we have to accept the situation, and be thankful that we can at least see them through his eyes, since otherwise we should know even less than we do.

Next in importance to Paul's writings we must place the Acts of the Apostles, a work which is later in date and presents an accommodation, not to say fusion, of Pauline Christianity and various forms of non-Pauline Christianity. The evidence of the Gospels and the remaining New Testament documents, as well as of other early Christian literature, must also be considered.

It is not the literature for its own sake that is studied in the following pages, however, but the leaders of early non-Pauline Christianity, with their associates, for whom the literature provides indispensable evidence.

CHAPTER 1

PETER AND THE ELEVEN

1. *Leader of the twelve*

It is clear from all four Gospels that, out of the wider circle of his followers, Jesus selected twelve men for special training, so that they might participate in his ministry and continue as his witnesses after his departure.[1] In some strands of the Synoptic record these twelve men are called "apostles".[2] This term, from the Greek *apostoloi*, "messengers", probably indicates that (like its supposed Hebrew counterpart *šelîḥîm*, "agents")[3] the people so designated were invested with their sender's authority for the discharge of their commission, that this authority was derived from him and was not intended to be inherent in themselves, and that it could not be transferred by them to others. Of the Synoptic evangelists it is Luke especially who uses this term

1. Cf. Matt. 10:1 ff.; Mark 3:14; Luke 6:13; John 6:67, 70.
2. Once in Matthew (10:2); once at least in Mark (6:30); repeatedly in Luke-Acts; never in John (ἀπόστολος in John 13:16 has the general sense "one who is sent").
3. For a recent discussion of the Hebrew term see C. K. Barrett, "Shaliah and Apostle", in *Donum Gentilicium: New Testament Studies in Honour of David Daube*, ed. E. Bammel, C. K. Barrett and W. D. Davies (Oxford, 1978), pp. 88–102.

of the twelve: in the Third Gospel and Acts it is applied almost exclusively to them.[4] At the beginning of his second volume Luke tells how, when their number had been reduced by one through the defection of Judas Iscariot, the others took steps to fill the vacancy and co-opted Matthias, who accordingly "was enrolled with the eleven apostles" (Acts 1:26).[5]

Of those twelve men Simon Peter was the acknowledged leader. There are differences between one evangelist and another in their portrayal of Peter,[6] but on this they are agreed.

Simon (or Symeon)[7] was his personal name: "Simon son of John" is the way Jesus addresses him in the Fourth Gospel (John 1:42; 21:15–17). In the form Simon Bar-Jona in Matt. 16:17, "Jona" (*Yōnā*) may well be an abridged form of *Yōḥānān*, "John", rather than the equivalent of the Hebrew name Jonah (*yōnāh*, "dove"). (Even less probable is the suggestion that Bar-Jona marks him out as a member of an insurgent faction.)[8]

4. The one exception is the double reference to Paul and Barnabas as ἀπόστολοι in Acts 14:4, 14 – perhaps with reference to their having been sent out from the church of Antioch (Acts 13:3 f.).

5. No such steps were taken when James the son of Zebedee was executed (Acts 12:2); James, having been faithful unto death, carried his apostleship into the life of the age to come, as Judas, because of his treachery, manifestly did not.

6. For a study of the varying portrayals of Peter in the four gospels, see R. E. Brown, K. P. Donfried, J. Reumann (ed.), *Peter in The New Testament* (New York, 1973), pp. 57–147.

7. "Symeon" in Acts 15:14 (see p. 38, n. 49); 2 Pet. 1:1 (Συμεὼν Πέτρος).

8. For this suggestion cf. R. Eisler, *The Messiah Jesus and John the Baptist* (London, 1931), pp. 252 ff. The *baryônîm* or *biryônîm* (an Akkadian loanword) were outlaws or terrorists; according to TB *Giṭṭin 56a* they gained control of the temple area during the first Jewish revolt against Rome, under the leadership of one Abba Siqera.

Peter (*Petros*) is the Greek form of the new name which Jesus gave him: "Simon he surnamed Peter" (Mark 3:16). Of the evangelists, John alone preserves the Aramaic form which Jesus actually used: when Andrew's brother was brought to Jesus, "Jesus looked at him, and said, 'So you are Simon the son of John? You shall be called *Kepha*'" (John 1:42).[9] The Aramaic form *Kepha* is not used by Matthew in his account of the confession at Caesarea Philippi, but it may readily be discerned behind the Greek *Petros* which Matthew uses: "You are Peter, and on this rock (*petra*) I will build my church" (Matt. 16:17). The Aramaic word, like its Hebrew counterpart *kēph* (Job 30:6; Jer. 4:29), means "rock"; in the Job targum from Qumran Cave 11 it is used twice as the rendering of Hebrew *sela'* ("rock" or "crag"), and it seems to have the same sense in several places in the Aramaic fragments of Enoch from Cave 4.[10] It appears as a personal name in the fifth century B.C. in one of the Jewish documents from Elephantine in Egypt.[11] Apart from its one occurrence in the Fourth Gospel, it appears several times in the writings of Paul, who habitually uses it in preference to the Greek form *Petros* when he refers to the leader of the twelve. Writing in Greek, both John and Paul supply the Aramaic word with the Greek

9. The narrator adds: "which means Peter (Πέτρος)". The commoner Greek equivalent of the Aramaic *kēphaʾ* would be the feminine πέτρα, but when it is given as a name to a man, the masculine form πέτρος must be used.

10. Cf. J. A. Fitzmyer, "Aramaic *Kephaʾ* and Peter's Name in the New Testament", in *Text and Interpretation: Studies in the New Testament presented to Matthew Black*, ed. E. Best and R. McL. Wilson (Cambridge, 1979), pp. 121–132.

11. Cf. E. G. Kraeling, *The Brooklyn Museum Aramaic Papyri* (New Haven, 1953), p. 227 (text 8, line 10).

masculine nominative termination, so that *Kepha*
becomes Kephas (Cephas in most English versions).

It is Peter who is said by Luke to have taken the
initiative in the arrangement to co-opt a replacement
for Judas Iscariot. It is Peter who, in the immediately
following account of the first Christian Pentecost,
stood up "with the eleven" and bore effective
witness to the resurrection of Christ in the hearing
of many visitors to Jerusalem (Acts 2:14 ff.). If it be
asked why the others acquiesced in Peter's leadership
so soon after the painful incident of his public denial
of Christ, the answer may lie in Peter's being the
first of the apostles to see the risen Christ: "the
Lord has risen indeed", they reported on the
evening of the first Easter Day, "and has appeared
to Simon!" (Luke 24:34).

What Luke implies in these words is confirmed in
Paul's earlier account: "Christ . . . was raised on the
third day in accordance with the scriptures, and
. . . appeared to Kephas, then to the twelve" (1 Cor.
15:3–5).

2. What became of the others?

At the beginning of his book *The Primitive Church*,
published in 1929, B. H. Streeter drew attention to
the question: "What became of the Twelve
Apostles?"[12] It is remarkable how difficult it is to
answer this question – the more remarkable when
we consider the important part which the twelve
play in the gospel record and the commission which
they are said to have received from the risen Christ,

12. B. H. Streeter, *The Primitive Church* (London, 1929), p. 3.

to be his witnesses and to win disciples for him among all nations.[13] Presumably they did in some degree fulfil their commission, but, so far as historical evidence goes, their fulfilment of it remains almost entirely unrecorded.

The second part of Luke's history of Christian beginnings does not really justify its traditional title, "The Acts of the Apostles" – still less the misnomer by which it is designated in the Muratorian canon at the end of the second century: "The Acts of *all* the Apostles".[14] The compiler of that canon probably had a dogmatic motive for his exaggeration, and a similar motive might perhaps be discerned behind the traditional title. The work in question relates, in fact, *some* acts of *some* apostles,[15] and to the missionary whose activities occupy most of its space, Paul, it does not give the title "apostle". (In the two places where the term *apostolos* is used of him in Acts, it is used in the plural, in reference to Barnabas and Paul together.)[16]

After the list of the eleven given at the beginning of Acts (1:13), only three of them are named again. Those three are Peter, James and John – the three who appear here and there in the Synoptic (in other words, the Markan) record as forming an inner group within the twelve. Legend is more than willing to tell us what happened to the others, as

13. Cf. Matt. 28:16–20; Luke 22:28–30; 24:44–49; John 17:18; 20:21–23. See p. 33 with n. 40.

14. Either he wished to rebut the Marcionite insistence on the solitary apostleship of Paul, or he wished to deny canonical status to the volumes of apostolic "Acts" which were beginning to proliferate in the second half of the second century.

15. This indeed is a possible rendering of its doubly anarthrous Greek title: Πράξεις Ἀποστόλων.

16. See p. 16, n. 4.

witness the various books of apocryphal "Acts" which appeared from the mid-second century onwards bearing the names of Andrew, Thomas and others, but it is extremely difficult to extract any historical data from them.

Of the three who receive further mention by name in the Lukan Acts, James the Zebedaean appears only in the account of his execution by Herod Agrippa I, somewhere in the period A.D. 41–44 (Acts 12:2). His brother John accompanies Peter at the healing of the cripple in the temple court at Jerusalem and their subsequent appearance before the Sanhedrin (Acts 3:1–4:22), and in the apostolic visitation to the Samaritans (Acts 8:14–25); after that he disappears from Luke's record. Much more is related of Peter in the early chapters of Acts, but he too disappears suddenly after his escape from Herod Agrippa's prison, when he announces his good news to the Christians who met in the house of Mary, John Mark's mother, and then goes "to another place" (Acts 12:6–17) – apart from his attendance at the Council of Jerusalem (Acts 15:7–14), which Luke places later but for which he depends on another source. (Let it be said here that when mention is made in these pages of Luke's "sources", the question whether oral or written sources of information are meant is left open.)

3. "Getting to know Kephas"

If we set Paul's references to Peter in what seems to be their historical sequence, the earliest is his statement in Gal. 1:18 that, three years after his conversion, he went up to Jerusalem (evidently from

Damascus), "to get to know Kephas".

This phrase (Greek *historēsai Kēphan*) has been much discussed.[17] Paul certainly wished to make Peter's acquaintance (which is the meaning of the verb *historeō* in Hellenistic Greek), but that was not his only purpose in paying his first post-conversion visit to Jerusalem. He wished also "to make enquiry" of Peter (which is the classical meaning of the verb), to obtain from him information which no one else was so well qualified to give. To obtain information from Peter was quite a different matter from receiving authority from him – Paul has just insisted that his gospel and his commission to preach it to the Gentiles were derived by him, without mediation, direct from the risen Lord.[18] But there was much that Peter could tell him – about the ministry and teaching of Jesus, for example, and in particular about his resurrection. Paul needed no one to tell him that Jesus was the risen Lord; he had learned this from his immediate confrontation with him on the Damascus road. He would certainly tell Peter how the risen Lord had appeared to him there,[19] but Peter could tell Paul how the same risen Lord had appeared earlier to *him*. When Paul reminds his Corinthian converts of the foundation facts of the gospel, including a summary of resurrection appearances, the first resurrection appearance which he mentions is that granted to Peter (1 Cor. 15:5). That

17. Cf. G. D. Kilpatrick, "Galatians 1:18 ἱστορῆσαι Κηφᾶν", in *New Testament Essays . . . in Memory of T. W. Manson*, ed. A. J. B. Higgins (Manchester, 1959), pp. 144–149; W. D. Davies, *The Setting of the Sermon on the Mount* (Cambridge, 1964), pp. 453–455, as well as commentaries on Galatians *ad loc.*

18. Gal. 1:11–17.

19. According to Acts 9:27 it was Barnabas who first told the apostles how Paul had seen and heard the Lord.

this information was obtained by Paul during his
first post-conversion visit to Jerusalem is not only
probable in itself; it is confirmed by the fact that the
only other named individual to whom he says the
risen Lord appeared (1 Cor. 15:7) is the only other
Jerusalem leader whom he claims to have met during
that visit (Gal. 1:19).[20]

After his appearance to Peter, the risen Lord
appeared to "the twelve" (1 Cor. 15:5), but the fact
that he appeared to Peter first is important; it may
(as has been suggested above) help to account for
the position of leadership which he occupied among
the apostles in the earliest days of the church. True,
he seems to have played a leading part among them
even during Jesus' ministry, but the others might
have felt that his denial of Jesus in the court of the
high priest's palace debarred him from any right to
exercise leadership thereafter.[21] All four of the
evangelists indicate in different ways that it was
nevertheless Jesus' will that Peter should be leader.
Mark relates how the women who went to the tomb
of Jesus early on Easter morning were directed to
"tell his disciples and Peter, 'He is going before you
to Galilee' " (Mark 16:7); the singling out of Peter
for special mention is significant. Matthew has the
saying, "You are Peter" (Matt. 16:18), found in no

20. James the Lord's brother; see pp. 88f.
21. The story of Peter's denial is assigned to an anti-Peter tradition by
G. Klein, "Die Verleugnung des Petrus", *ZTK* 58 (1961), pp. 285–328,
reprinted in *Rekonstruktion und Interpretation* (Munich, 1969), pp. 49–98.
E. Linnemann, criticizing Klein's thesis, treats the story as an indivi-
dualization of the denial of all the disciples, "Die Verleugnung des
Petrus", *ZTK* 63 (1966), pp. 1–32, reprinted in *Studien zur Passionsge-
schichte* (Göttingen, 1970), pp. 70–108. Klein defends his thesis against
her towards the end of "Die Berufung des Petrus", *ZNW* 58 (1967), pp.
1–44, reprinted in *Rekonstruktion und Interpretation*, pp. 11–48.

other gospel; there may be symbolical meaning too in the incident (also peculiar to Matthew) of Peter's being grasped by Jesus and brought to safety when he was "beginning to sink" (Matt. 14:28–32). Luke tells how Jesus forewarned Peter of his failure but added, "I have prayed for you that your faith may not fail; and when you have turned again, strengthen your brethren" (Luke 22:31 f.). Finally, John has his epilogue in which, after the resurrection, Peter is commissioned afresh by Jesus beside Lake Tiberias to be the shepherd of his flock (John 21:15–17).[22]

In later days the story of Peter's rehabilitation and restoration, not only to discipleship but to leadership, in spite of his ignominious denial of his Lord, lent itself as a weighty precedent for those who believed that Christians who denied Christ or forswore their faith in time of persecution might nevertheless, after due penitence, be restored to communion. If the policy of the rigorists, who admitted no hope of restoration for the lapsed, had prevailed in Peter's case, the course of primitive Christianity would have been quite other than it actually was.[23]

4. The Acts of Peter

Here it is convenient to turn again to the early chapters of Acts. Apart from the Hellenistic sections (Acts 6:1–8:40; 11:19–26) and the narrative of Paul's conversion (Acts 9:1–31, to which the references to his persecuting activity in 7:58b and 8:3 provide an

22. This theme is taken up in the exhortation to fellow-elders in 1 Pet. 5:1–4.
23. Cf. G. W. H. Lampe, "St. Peter's Denial", *BJRL* 55 (1972–73), pp. 346–368.

introduction), the first twelve chapters of the book are dominated by Peter. There is, indeed, much to be said for the view that those chapters present the reader with "Acts of Peter" designedly parallel to the "Acts of Paul" in the later part of the book.[24]

We have mentioned Peter's taking the initiative in the replacement of Judas (Acts 1:15–26) and in the public witness on the day of Pentecost (Acts 2:14 ff.). Although he is accompanied by John on the visit to the temple when the lame man was healed at the Beautiful Gate, it is Peter who addresses the crowd which was attracted by the miraculous healing (Acts 3:12–26). If the sermon on the day of Pentecost and that in the temple court are derived from two distinct Jerusalem sources, as Harnack and others have thought,[25] then the prominence which Luke gives to Peter has its foundation in pre-Lukan tradition. When Peter and John are consequently arrested for causing a disturbance, it is Peter who makes the speech for the defence before the Sanhedrin (Acts 4:8–12). When Ananias and Sapphira bring the apostles part of the proceeds from the sale of their land, pretending to hand over the whole amount, it is at Peter's rebuke that they fall down dead, the one after the other (Acts 5:1–11). Such is Peter's prestige in Jerusalem that people believe that his very shadow will cure their sick folk. In Acts 8:15–25 Peter and John visit Samaria in the aftermath of Philip's mission and lay their hands on the

24. Cf. M. Schneckenburger, *Ueber den Zweck der Apostelgeschichte* (Bern, 1841), pp. 52–55; R. B. Rackham, *The Acts of the Apostles* (London, 1901), pp. xlvii–xlix.

25. A Harnack, *The Acts of the Apostles,* E. T. (London, 1909), pp. 179–195; cf. J. Dupont, *The Sources of Acts,* E. T. (London, 1964), pp. 33–61.

converts so that they receive the Holy Spirit. But John is still very much of a lay figure; it is Peter who rebukes Simon Magus for his "simony".[26]

Later, Peter embarks on a preaching and healing tour outside Jerusalem, in the area between the capital and the Mediterranean coast. He cures a paralytic at Lydda (Acts 9:32–35) and restores a Christian woman to life at Joppa (9:36–42); as a result, the groups of disciples already resident there are greatly augmented.

The great leap forward then takes place: Peter, who opened a door of faith to Jews on the day of Pentecost, now performs the same service for Gentiles (Acts 10:34–48). He is fetched from Joppa to present the gospel to the Roman centurion Cornelius and his household. Cornelius is depicted as a God-fearer, but he was still a Gentile. Only under an irresistible persuasion of divine constraint did Peter accept the invitation to enter Cornelius's house, but the sequel fully confirmed the rightness of his doing so: the same tokens of the gift of the Spirit were manifested in those Gentiles when they believed Peter's message as had been manifested in the Jews who believed at Pentecost. Presented with this divine *fait accompli*, Peter directed that the new converts should be baptized.

The chronological relation between Peter's preaching to Cornelius at Caesarea and the evangelization of Gentiles at Antioch by unknown Hellenists (Acts

---

26. The Lukan account of Peter's confrontation with Simon Magus (Acts 8:18–24) provides the archetype for later descriptions of confrontations between the two, as in the *Acts of Peter* (4 ff.) and the Pseudo-Clementines (*Recognitions* 1:72 ff.; *Homilies* 16: 1 ff.). See pp. 116f. with nn. 54, 56, 58.

11:19–21) cannot be determined;[27] the two narratives were derived by Luke from different sources. But Luke evidently gives priority to Peter's action: not only does he relate it before the other but at the Council of Jerusalem he represents Peter as claiming by implication that it was from his mouth that Gentiles first heard the gospel (Acts 15:7).

Peter's fellow-apostles were at first disturbed by the report of his action, but they acquiesced in it when they heard his own account, acknowledging that he had no option in the matter (Acts 11:1–18). His action and their acquiescence, however, had an unforeseen sequel.

Herod Agrippa, grandson of Herod the Great, whom the Emperor Gaius had invested in A.D. 37 with a grant of territory in the north of Palestine and the title king, had his territory increased by Claudius in A.D. 41 when Judaea was transferred from its provincial status to become part of Herod's kingdom. The church of Jerusalem and her daughter-churches in Judaea now found themselves under his rule, and for them his rule was unfriendly. Rabbinical tradition suggests that Herod set himself sedulously to court the good will of the Jewish religious establishment.[28] By this time the Jewish religious establishment had not only taken up a hostile attitude to the Jerusalem church; it found itself supported by a wider body of the Judaean public in this hostility so far as it was directed against one section of the church – the section led by Peter and the other apostles.

So much we gather from Luke's statement that,

27. See pp. 60ff.
28. Cf. Mishnah, tractate *Bikkurim* 3:4; *Soṭah* 7:8.

after arresting and executing James the Zebedaean, Herod, seeing "that it pleased the Jews", went on to arrest and imprison Peter (Acts 12:3). James the Zebedaean was a leader among the twelve, but not *the* leader. Herod might not have ventured to attack Peter until he saw what the public reaction was to his action against James. The statement that his action "pleased the Jews" might be put down – indeed, it has been put down – to an anti-Jewish tendency on Luke's part, but there are some elements in the context which encourage us to think that Luke's statement accurately represents the situation. Herod, says Luke, "laid violent hands upon some who belonged to the church" (Acts 12:1) – not on the church as a whole. Luke, or his source, is evidently aware that only part of the church was the target for Herod's attack.

In an earlier outbreak of persecution – that which followed Stephen's execution – it was primarily, though not exclusively, the Hellenists in the church who were attacked.[29] The apostles are specifically said to have been immune (Acts 8:1). Why then, only ten or twelve years later, should the apostles become the principal target of attack? The answer, in all probability, is to be found in Peter's recent fraternizing with Gentiles – members of the Roman army of occupation at that – and in the other apostles' approval of his action. Such an action could not have commended itself to the majority of religious Jews in Jerusalem. Herod, of course, had no personal objection to fraternizing with Gentiles

29. See pp. 57f. Whatever Luke may imply, Paul makes no distinctions when he tells how he "persecuted the church" (1 Cor. 15:9; Gal. 1:13; Phil. 3:6).

– was he not a long-standing friend of the Emperor
Claudius? – but he knew what was expected of him
in Judaea and, now that the apostles had forfeited
public good will, he could proceed against them
without fear.

Herod, then, imprisoned Peter just before Passover, intending to have him publicly executed when
the week's festival of Unleavened Bread was past.
But Peter was enabled to escape from prison and,
after announcing his escape to the disciples who met
in Mary's house, and who at that very time were
praying for his release, he left for an unknown
destination, bidding them give the news of his
escape "to James and to the brethren" (Acts 12:17)
– that is, the brethren associated with James the
Lord's brother (commonly called James the Just),
whose meeting-place was evidently somewhere else.
This is the first indication given by Luke that there
was a group in the Jerusalem church which looked
to this James as its leader.[30]

5. Conference at Jerusalem

We go back now to Paul's narrative. After the
fifteen days' visit to Peter recorded in Gal. 1:18, Paul
went to Syria and Cilicia and did not see Peter again
for fourteen, or at least eleven, years. (It is uncertain
whether the phrase "after fourteen years" in Gal.
2:1 denotes fourteen years from his previous visit or
fourteen years from his conversion.)[31] In either case,

30. See pp. 88, 91.
31. Cf. G. Ogg, *The Chronology of the Life of Paul* (London, 1968), pp.
56 f., for the view (preferable, as I think) that the fourteen years date
from his conversion.

when Paul went to Jerusalem next, Herod Agrippa's death would already have taken place (A.D. 44) and Peter could come out of hiding and move about freely in Jerusalem.

On this second post-conversion visit by Paul to Jerusalem, he and Barnabas (who accompanied him from Antioch) had a private conference with the leaders of the Jerusalem church. One purpose of the conference was apparently the demarcation of the mission-fields of Paul and Barnabas on the one hand and of the Jerusalem leaders on the other. The Jerusalem leaders are named by Paul as "James and Kephas and John" (Gal. 2:9). The order in which they are named is probably significant.[32] On Paul's previous visit to Jerusalem Peter was the important man, the man whom Paul had to meet. Incidentally, almost, he mentions that he also saw James. Now James evidently takes precedence over the two leading survivors of the twelve – even over Peter. It may be that James's authority had been enhanced by Peter's absence from the scene after his escape from Herod Agrippa's prison. The three leaders with whom Paul and Barnabas conferred are said by Paul to have been reputed as "pillars" in the mother-church: the figure of speech suggests that they were regarded as pillars in the true, spiritual temple of God, the new temple not made with hands.[33]

The outcome of the conference, according to Paul, was the Jerusalem leaders' recognition that he was

32. See p. 90 with n. 7. It is probably no more than a coincidence that, in the traditional sequence of the catholic epistles, those of James, Peter and John appear in that order.

33. Cf. C. K. Barrett, "Paul and the 'Pillar' Apostles", in *Studia Paulina in honorem J. de Zwaan*, ed. J. N. Sevenster and W. C. van Unnik (Haarlem, 1953), pp. 1–19.

as truly commissioned to evangelize Gentiles as Peter was to evangelize Jews, and an agreement that Paul and Barnabas should concentrate on the Gentile mission while the Jerusalem leaders prosecuted the mission to Jews. Indeed, at one point in Paul's report it has been thought that he reproduces something like the official minutes of the agreement,[34] for at this point he departs from his regular practice of calling the prince of the apostles Kephas and refers to him twice as Peter (*Petros*): "they saw", he says, "that I had been entrusted with the gospel to the uncircumcised, just as Peter had been entrusted with the gospel to the circumcised, for he who worked through Peter for the mission to the circumcised worked through me also for the Gentiles" (Gal. 2:7 f.).

If Paul is indeed dependent here on someone else's report, he integrates it with its autobiographical context by substituting the pronoun of the first person singular for his own name. Then he repeats the substance of the agreement in his own words, reverting to the form Kephas: "When they perceived the grace that was given to me, James and Kephas and John, men of repute as 'pillars', gave to me and Barnabas the right hand of fellowship, that we should go to the Gentiles and they to the circumcised" (Gal. 2:9).[35]

There is no hint of any difference in content between the gospel which the Jerusalem leaders

---

34. Cf. E. Dinkler, "Der Brief an die Galater", in *Verkündigung und Forschung* (1953–55), pp. 182 f.; "Die Petrus-Rom-Frage", *Theologische Rundschau* 25 (1959), p. 198.

35. Cf. G. Klein, "Galater 2, 6–9 und die Geschichte der Jerusalemer Urgemeinde", *ZTK* 57 (1960), pp. 275–295, reprinted in *Rekonstruktion und Interpretation*, pp. 99–128.

were to preach to the Jews and Paul and Barnabas to the Gentiles. As Paul said elsewhere with regard to the basic facts of the gospel, "Whether then it was I or they [the Jerusalem leaders], so we preach and so you [the Corinthian Christians] believed" (1 Cor. 15:11). Differences of emphasis and approach there would certainly have been, but the Jerusalem leaders seem to have raised no objection to the gospel which Paul preached among the Gentiles and which he laid before them on this occasion (Gal. 2:2).[36]

It is possible that the agreement about the delimitation of the two mission-fields concealed ambiguities which did not come to light until the agreement began to be worked out in practice. When they did come to light, various tensions were set up. We have some idea how Paul understood the agreement; we could wish that we had independent information about Peter's understanding of it, or indeed that we had an account of the conference from Peter as well as from Paul.

For example, was the delimitation to be interpreted geographically or communally? Either way, it must have been difficult to define the boundaries of the two mission-fields. Jews and Gentiles were to be found in almost every large city of the eastern Mediterranean world. It is unlikely that Paul felt himself debarred by the agreement from visiting synagogues in Gentile cities. We have his own word

36. Even between Paul and those against whom he polemicizes in Galatians, says J. D. G. Dunn, "what was at issue . . . was not the traditional formulation of the gospel, but Paul's *interpretation* of it" (*Unity and Diversity in the New Testament* [London, 1977], p. 66) – not the basic facts, but the terms on which their saving efficacy should be received. See also G. Howard. *Paul: Crisis in Galatia* (Cambridge, 1979), pp. 20–45.

for it that, while he knew himself called to be
apostle to the Gentiles, he followed the Jewish way
of life when he found himself in Jewish company,
"in order to win Jews" for the gospel (1 Cor. 9:20).
There is no reason to doubt the testimony of Acts
which depicts him as entering the synagogue in one
city after another to which he came and finding the
nucleus of the church which he planted in such a
city among the God-fearing Gentiles who frequented
the synagogue.[37]

Equally, it is unlikely that Peter felt himself
debarred from evangelizing the Jews of (say) Corinth
or Rome. But since the churches eventually established in those cities comprised both Jewish and
Gentile converts, some dovetailing or overlapping of
the two spheres of missionary activity was inevitable.

That Peter's missionary activity was not restricted
to Jews is implied here and there in the New
Testament. Whatever view be taken of the life-setting
of 1 Peter, that letter is addressed in Peter's name
to Gentile converts in various provinces of Asia
Minor (including two which were evangelized by
Paul).[38] The terminology proper to the old Israel is
taken over and applied to these new "exiles of the
Dispersion", but their pagan background is not left
in doubt.[39]

37. W. Schmithals agrees that Paul endeavoured to establish contact
with God-fearers in each place but denies that he preached in
synagogues to do so: accounts of his synagogue ministry are purely
Lukan constructions (*Paul and James*, E.T. [London, 1965], pp. 60 f.).

38. Cf. C. J. Hemer, "The Address of 1 Peter", *The Expository Times*
89 (1977–78), pp. 239–243.

39. The letter comprises an exhortation on Christian living in a pagan
society, suitable for new converts on the occasion of their baptism
(1:3–4:11), followed by encouragement in face of persecution (4:12–5:11).
In the former part, suffering for righteousness' sake is mentioned as a

Again, the first evangelist records a commission given by the risen Christ to the eleven (Peter, of course, included) to "go . . . and make disciples of all the nations (Gentiles)" and in particular to teach them to observe "all that I have commanded you" (Matt. 28:19 f.). We must come to terms with the fact that Paul represents Peter as agreeing to a drastic limitation of the commission which, according to Matthew, Peter and his colleagues had received from their Lord.[40]

The early Christian document called the *Didache*, which leans heavily on the Gospel of Matthew, is so called because it claims to set forth "the Lord's teaching (*didachē*) to the Gentiles through the twelve apostles" – the apostle to the Gentiles *par excellence* being rather pointedly left out of the picture. There was, in fact, a strand in early Christianity which did not take Paul's Gentile apostolate seriously and regarded the evangelization of Gentiles as the responsibility *and achievement* of the twelve. We may recall further that, in the apocalyptic vision of the new Jerusalem, the city's twelve foundation-stones are inscribed with "the twelve names of the twelve

---

remote contingency (3:13); in the latter, suffering for the profession of Christianity is an imminent certainty (4:16). A suitable life-setting would be the outbreak of persecution of Roman Christians in A.D. 64/65, in which it was to be expected that "the same experience of suffering" would be "required of the brotherhood throughout the world" (5:9). The letter is sent in the name of Peter (1:1) by the hand of Silvanus (5:12).

40. This was acknowledged by such a champion of orthodoxy as Sir Robert Anderson. Regarding Matt. 28:19 he wrote: "The fact that the commission there recorded remained a dead letter is wrongly used to discredit the authenticity of the words. That the commission was not acted on by the Apostles is clear to every student of the Acts" (*The Buddha of Christendom* [London, 1899], p. 270). He foresaw the fulfilment of the commission in a day yet future. (See p. 19, n. 13.)

apostles of the Lamb" (Rev. 21:14).

At any rate, full mutual confidence between the
contracting parties at the Jerusalem conference was
essential if the agreement was to work amicably and
effectively. And before long something happened
which shook this mutual confidence.

6. Confrontation at Antioch

Some time after the conference in Jerusalem, Paul
tells us, Peter visited Antioch. Paul's account of
Peter's behaviour at Antioch – enjoying table-fellowship happily with Jewish and Gentile Christians alike
– agrees with Luke's account of the lesson which
Peter took to heart in connexion with his visit to
Cornelius: that he should not call any one "common
or unclean" (Acts 10:28). If Peter accepted the
hospitality of Gentiles at Caesarea, even to the point
of eating with them, he was equally ready to do so
at Antioch.

During his visit to Antioch, then, all went well
until, says Paul, some people[41] arrived from Jerusalem, sent by James. After their arrival, Peter with-
drew from table-fellowship with Gentile Christians
and ate with Jewish Christians only. In Paul's eyes,
this was a piece of play-acting, because Peter had
no conscientious scruples about eating with Gentiles.
Peter's example, moreover, was followed by other
Jewish Christians there; worst of all, it was followed
even by Barnabas. The effect of this action on

---

41. The variant reading τινα, "some one" (P^{46} etc.) for τινας, "some
people", is best explained as "the result of scribal oversight" (B. M.
Metzger, *A Textual Commentary on the Greek New Testament* [London/New
York, 1971], p. 592).

Gentile Christians must have been devastating; they must have felt themselves relegated to the status of second-class citizens in the church, with no hope of attaining first-class status except by submitting to circumcision. Paul, concerned for the Gentile Christians, delivered a public rebuke to Peter (Gal. 2:11–14).

But what made Peter act as he did? What did the messengers from James say to him?

They may have said something like this: "News is reaching us in Jerusalem that you are habitually practising table-fellowship with Gentiles. This is causing grave scandal to our more conservative brethren here. Not only so; it is becoming common knowledge outside the church, and is seriously hampering our attempts to evangelize our fellow-Jews."[42]

But this would scarcely satisfy Paul's language when he says that Peter "separated himself, fearing the circumcision party" (Gal. 2:12). Perhaps James's messengers had a more serious report to give to Peter. The mid-forties witnessed a revival of militancy among Judaean freedom-fighters. It was about this time that repressive action was taken against them by Tiberius Julius Alexander, procurator of Judaea, who crucified two of their leaders, Jacob and Simon, sons of that Judas who had led the revolt against the census in A.D. 6.[43] In the eyes of such militants, Jews who fraternized with the uncircumcised were no better than traitors, and the leaders

---

42. Cf. T. W. Manson, "The Problem of the Epistle to the Galatians", *BJRL* 24 (1940), pp. 69–72, reprinted in *Studies in the Gospels and Epistles* (Manchester, 1962), pp. 178–181.

43. Josephus, *Ant.* 20.102.

of the Jerusalem church may have felt themselves
endangered by the reports of Peter's free-and-easy
conduct at Antioch.[44] Whatever the precise terms of
the message were, Peter took it seriously enough to
discontinue eating with Gentile Christians – for the
time being, at least.

Here again we find ourselves wishing that we had
Peter's account of the matter. But in fact it is not
too difficult to imagine how he would have defended
his action. He would have claimed that he acted out
of consideration for weaker brethren – the weaker
brethren on this occasion being those back home in
Jerusalem. Tertullian appears to have seen this: he
goes so far as to suggest that it was Paul's
immaturity that made him so critical of Peter. Later
on, he points out, Paul himself "was to become in
practice all things to all men, to those under the
law, as under the law" (1 Cor. 9:20).[45] The trouble
was that Peter's concern for the weaker brethren in
Jerusalem conflicted with Paul's concern for the
Gentile brethren in Antioch, the more so since
Peter's action seemed to Paul to compromise the
principles of the gospel on which, he thought, both
sides had agreed at the Jerusalem conference. Paul
would go far enough out of consideration for weaker
brethren, but not so far as to countenance separate
tables, for this was in practice to undo the unity
which Christ had effected between Jewish and
Gentile believers.

Again, Tertullian suggests that, "since Paul himself
became 'all things to all men, so that he might win

---

44. Cf. R. Jewett, "The Agitators and the Galatian Congregation",
NTS 17 (1970–71), pp. 198–212.
45. *Against Marcion* 1.20.

them all', Peter too may well have had this in mind when he acted in some respect differently from his manner of teaching".[46] That Peter had some reason on his side was felt by Barnabas who, as we have seen, followed Peter's example. Confidence between Paul and Peter (and even between Paul and Barnabas) was shaken and perhaps never fully restored.

Some scholars have suggested that what Peter did (at James's behest) was to try to impose on the Gentile Christians of Antioch the terms of the decree agreed upon at the Council of Jerusalem, according to the record of Acts 15:22–29.[47] It seems more probable to me that the Council of Jerusalem was held as a sequel to the confrontation at Antioch, and that an attempt to impose its decree on Pauline churches was made rather later, and possibly in Peter's name.[48]

It is tempting to identify the messengers from James with the men who, according to Acts 15:1, came down to Antioch from Judaea and taught the Gentile Christians that, unless they were circumcised "according to the custom of Moses", they could not be saved. More probably, however, the men of Acts 15:1 are to be identified with the infiltrating "false brethren" of Gal. 2:4 who first, according to Paul, insisted that Gentile Christians ought to be circumcised.

46. *Against Marcion* 4.3.

47. Cf. D. W. B. Robinson, "The Circumcision of Titus and Paul's 'Liberty' ", *Australian Biblical Review* 12 (1964), pp. 40 f.; D. R. Catchpole, "Paul, James and the Apostolic Decree", *NTS* 23 (1976–77), pp. 442 f. Pointing out that Paul utters no criticism of James in Gal. 2:11 ff., G. Howard hazards the conjecture "that James understood Paul's gospel better than Peter and in fact was closer to Paul in theology than Peter" (*Paul: Crisis in Galatia*, p. 79).

48. See p. 41, n. 55.

However that may be, the church of Jerusalem was sufficiently concerned about the issue to give careful consideration to the conditions on which table-fellowship between Jewish and Gentile Christians might be allowed. It was resolved, against some opposition, that circumcision should not be required. According to Luke, a powerful plea by Peter was specially influential in the achieving of this resolution.[49] Luke's account of the part played by Peter on this occasion is not at all inconsistent with what is otherwise known of his outlook: "the figure of a Judaizing St. Peter is a figment of the Tübingen critics with no basis in history."[50] James the Just, who summed up the sense of the meeting, took his cue from Peter's plea. The letter to the Gentile churches of Syria and Cilicia (i.e. Antioch and her daughter-churches) which embodied the resolution, went on to stipulate that Gentile Christians should conform to the main Jewish food-laws (in particular, the avoidance of blood and the rejection of idolatrous meat) and to the Jewish code of relations between the sexes. These stipulations constitute what is commonly called the Jerusalem decree or the apostolic decree.[51] In the decision not to require circum-

49. Paul himself could scarcely have put the case for gospel liberty more powerfully than Peter does in Acts 15:7–11; to impose on Gentile converts conditions which God had not required is described by Peter as "tempting God" – language similar to that used in the case of Ananias and Sapphira (Acts 5:9). The statement that Peter's speech influenced the decision of the council would be invalidated if from verse 13 onwards Luke draws on a source which described a later meeting (with verse 12 providing the transition between his two sources), the meeting described in verses 6–11 being that of Gal. 2:1–10. I cannot identify the meeting of Acts 15:6–11 with that of Gal. 2:1–10; for one thing, they dealt with two distinct issues. See p. 103, n. 31.

50. K. Lake, *The Earlier Epistles of St. Paul* (London, ²1914), p. 116.

51. The decree is proposed by James in Acts 15:20 and embodied in

cision Martin Hengel sees evidence of "an astound-
ing magnanimity" on the part of the Jerusalem
leaders, for "this bold step necessarily meant defa-
mation for them and persecution by the Jewish
majority in Palestine".[52]

7. Peter's wider ministry

Peter receives no further mention in Acts. Henceforth, therefore, our attempt to trace his subsequent
career becomes specially interesting, because we have
to piece together a few fragments of a jigsaw puzzle
and use a lively (and, it is hoped, disciplined)
imagination to envisage the picture as a whole.

Such evidence as we have suggests that, from
about mid-century on, Peter engaged in a fairly
wide-ranging ministry and was no longer regularly
resident in Jerusalem. Our principal evidence from
this period comes from Paul's Corinthian correspondence. Paul came to Corinth in the later summer of
A.D. 50 and in the course of eighteen months built
up a vigorous, if volatile, church in that city. From
there he moved to Ephesus, and from time to time
during his Ephesian ministry he received visitors
from Corinth who carried back messages or letters
from him to the Corinthian church. Early in A.D. 55
he received visitors who brought what for him was
the disquieting news that factions, or at least rival
schools of thought, were developing in the Corinthian church, each invoking some outstanding name

the apostolic letter in Acts 15:28 f. (see p. 92 with n. 12). Paul is
informed (reminded?) of it in Acts 21:25, when he pays his last visit to
Jerusalem (see p. 107).

52. M. Hengel, *Victory over Violence*, E. T. (London, 1975), p. 87.

(1 Cor. 1:12). The members of one faction, no doubt
out of a sense of loyalty to Paul, called themselves
his followers; one of the other parties claimed Peter
as its leader: "I belong to Kephas", a member of
this party would say.

But why should a group of Corinthian Christians
claim Peter as their leader? We know that another
group invoked the name of Apollos, but then we
know that Apollos actually visited Corinth after
Paul's departure and made a great impression there.[53]
It is conceivable that some visitors from Judaea or
Syria, invoking Peter's name and authority, had tried
to impose their particular understanding of Christian
faith and life on the church of Corinth; but since
the two other men who were set up as party-leaders
– Paul and Apollos – had actually been present in
Corinth, it is probable that Peter had visited the city
in person. This conclusion is supported by a passage
later in 1 Corinthians where Paul speaks of certain
rights to which, as an apostle, he would certainly be
entitled, but which he chose to forgo, such as the
right to marry and take his wife around with him
on his missionary journeys, expecting the churches
to support her as well as himself, like "the other
apostles and the brothers of the Lord and Kephas"
(1 Cor. 9:5). Why does he name "Kephas" separately
from "the other apostles"? Not because he did not
include him among the apostles (a view which has
actually been defended) but because the Corinthian
Christians had actually seen Peter, and his wife too,
on a visit to their city.

If we try to discover the distinctive features of the

53. 1 Cor. 3:5 f.; Acts 18:27 f.; see pp. 65 ff.

party which claimed the leadership of Peter, we may not be far wrong in thinking that it was marked by a fairly strict adherence to the stipulations of the Jerusalem decree. The content of those stipulations would not have been unacceptable to Paul. That dealing with relations between the sexes he would have regarded as part of the order of creation. As for those relating to food, he himself urged that in such matters the scruples of fellow-Christians should be considered. But such consideration should be spontaneous, not enforced. For example, one question on which the Corinthian church sought a ruling from Paul concerned the flesh of animals which had been sacrificed to pagan divinities. The Jerusalem decree had enjoined abstention from such food, but in answering the Corinthians' question Paul made no reference to the decree. He wished his converts to be guided by Christian love, not by the decisions of the mother-church. Food was religiously indifferent: what mattered was the effect that one's taking it might have on the conscience of a more immature or less enlightened fellow-Christian.[54]

There is no reason to think that Peter would not have agreed with Paul in principle, but it would not be surprising if the party that invoked his authority held that the Jerusalem decree should be accepted as binding.[55]

It is difficult to be sure if Peter was one of the "superlative apostles" whose prestige was made much of by later visitors to the Corinthian church (2 Cor. 11:5; 12:11) and whose status, it was

---

54. 1 Cor. 8:1–12; 10:14–33 (cf. Rom. 14:1–15.3).
55. Cf. C. K. Barrett, "Things Sacrificed to Idols", *NTS* 11 (1964–65), pp. 138–153, especially pp. 149 f.

maintained, was so much higher than Paul's that he was a mere nobody in comparison with them. Those visitors themselves preached a non-Pauline version of Christianity, or rather a perversion, as Paul reckoned it, to the point where he denounces its preachers as "false apostles" (2 Cor. 11:13). But even if Peter was one of the "superlative apostles" to whose authority they appealed, he cannot be held in any way responsible for their "different gospel" (2 Cor. 11:4).

A Paulinist (and I myself must be so described) is under a constant temptation to underestimate Peter. For example, when A. S. Peake delivered his presidential address to the 1928 assembly of the National Free Church Council, on "The Reunion of the Christian Churches", he referred to the claims of the Roman see in these words: "I have no wish to rob Peter to pay Paul – Peter indeed cannot so well afford it – but I am certainly not going to rob Paul to pay Peter."[56] The parenthesis – "Peter indeed cannot so well afford it" – came no doubt naturally to the lips of such a devoted Paulinist as Peake was but, even if the Roman see was uppermost in his mind, his words may do the historical Peter an injustice.

An impressive tribute is paid to Peter by Dr. J. D. G. Dunn towards the end of his *Unity and Diversity in the New Testament.* Contemplating the diversity within the New Testament canon, he thinks of the compilation of the canon as an exercise in bridge-building, and suggests that "it was Peter who became the focal point of unity in the great Church,

56. A. S. Peake, *Plain Thoughts on Great Subjects* (London, 1931), pp. 43 f.

since *Peter was probably in fact and effect the bridge-man who did more than any other to hold together the diversity of first-century Christianity*".[57] Paul and James, he thinks, were too much identified in the eyes of many Christians with this and that extreme of the spectrum to fill the rôle that Peter did. Consideration of Dr. Dunn's thoughtful words has moved me to think more highly of Peter's contribution to the early church, without at all diminishing my estimate of Paul's contribution.

8. *Antioch, Corinth and Rome*

There are three places in the Mediterranean world with which Peter's name is specially associated. Antioch and Corinth have already been mentioned; the third is Rome.

In none of these places was Peter directly associated with the founding of the church; yet such was the prestige of his name that all three laid claim to him as apostolic founder – in partnership with Paul.

Thus, in the fourth-century *Apostolic Constitutions*, the first two post-apostolic bishops of Antioch are said to have been Euodius, ordained by Peter, and then Ignatius, ordained by Paul.[58] These two ordinations are quite unhistorical, but they reflect the

57. J. D. G. Dunn, *Unity and Diversity in the New Testament* (London, 1977), p. 385 (his italics). The bridge-building quality of the canon is illustrated by the fact that in 2 Peter, generally held to be the latest document in the canon, Peter appears as a personal witness to the divine attestation of Jesus as the Son of God (1:16–18) and "as an authority who can correct misinterpretations of Paul (3:14–16)" (R. E. Brown, etc., *Peter in the New Testament* [New York, 1973], p. 17). On Peter see also F. J. Foakes-Jackson, *Peter: Prince of Apostles* (London, 1927) and O. Cullmann, *Peter: Disciple – Apostle – Martyr*, E. T. (London, [2]1962).
58. *Apostolic Constitutions* 7.46.

desire of the church of Antioch to make the most of
the two apostles who, for a shorter or longer period,
were present with it in its early days.

Even more remarkably, Dionysius, bishop of Corinth, writing to the bishop of Rome about A.D. 170,
refers to the Roman church's claim to have been
founded by Peter and Paul and makes a similar
claim for his own church: "for both of them taught
together in this Corinth of ours and were *our*
founders".[59] Paul would certainly have disclaimed
any part in the planting of the Roman church,
which he recognized to be "another man's foundation"[60] (Rom. 15:20), but what he would have
thought of the suggestion – made by a Corinthian
bishop, forsooth – that Peter was joint-founder with
him of the church of Corinth taxes one's imagination!

As for Peter's association with the Roman church,
this was not only a claim made from early days at
Rome; it was conceded by churchmen from all over
the Christian world. In the New Testament it is
reflected in the greetings sent to the readers of 1
Peter from the church (literally, from "her") "that is
in Babylon, elect together with you" (1 Pet. 5:13) –
if, as is most probable, Babylon is a code-word for
Rome.[61]

The gospel appears to have found a lodgement in
Rome before the expulsion of Jews from the capital
by the edict of Claudius about A.D. 49. Paul's

59. Eusebius, *Hist. Eccl.* 2.25.8.

60. The wording, ἐπ' ἀλλότριον θεμέλιον, does not necessarily imply
that Paul had a particular individual in mind as the "other man".

61. Various considerations rule out Babylon on the Euphrates. A case
has sometimes been presented for the Roman military settlement at
Babylon on the Nile (Old Cairo); cf. G. T. Manley, "Babylon on the
Nile", *EQ* 16 (1944), pp. 138–146.

friends, Priscilla and Aquila, who were expelled at that time, seem to have been Christians before they met Paul in Corinth the following year. By the time of Claudius's death in A.D. 54 the expulsion edict had become a dead letter: Jews were soon as numerous in Rome as ever they had been. As for the Christian community in Rome, comprising Jewish, Gentile and (probably) mixed house-churches, it was large and flourishing by the time it received Paul's epistle in A.D. 57.

A visit to Rome by Peter (perhaps accompanied by Mark) would have helped to give fresh impetus to Christianity in the capital when it revived after the expulsion edict. We have no direct evidence for this, but such a visit has been postulated on independent grounds by various scholars. The Bampton lecturer for 1913, for example, argued cogently that Peter's brief visit to Corinth (implied in 1 Corinthians) was paid when he was on the way to Rome to help with the reconstruction of the church there, after receiving news of Claudius's death in October, A.D. 54.[62] T. W. Manson, examining the early *testimonia* for the genesis of the Gospel of Mark, interpreted them thus:

> If Peter had paid a visit to Rome some time between 55 and 60; if Mark had been his interpreter then; if after Peter's departure from the city Mark had taken in hand – at the request of the Roman hearers – a written record of what Peter had said; then the essential points

62. G. Edmundson, *The Church in Rome in the First Century* (London, 1913), pp. 80, 84. The first Roman church is supposed to have practically disappeared through Claudius's expulsion of Jews about A.D. 49 (see p. 72 below).

in the evidence would all be satisfied.[63]

For my part, I prefer to link the composition of Mark's Gospel with the persecution of Roman Christians which followed the great fire of July, A.D. 64.[64] It is this persecution which provides a suitable life-setting for the one really indubitable event of Peter's association with Rome – his death there. This event may justly be called indubitable because, in Hans Lietzmann's words:

> All the early sources about the year 100 become clear and easily intelligible, and agree with their historical context and with each other, if we accept what they plainly suggest to us – namely, that Peter sojourned in Rome and died a martyr there. Any other hypothesis regarding Peter's death piles difficulty upon difficulty, and cannot be supported by a single document.[65]

The claim that Peter and Paul were joint-founders of the Roman church – attested, as we have seen, by Dionysius of Corinth – is earlier than the tracing of the succession of bishops of Rome back to them, which is first attested in Irenaeus but may go back to Hegesippus.[66] Strictly, Peter was no more founder of the Roman church than Paul was, but in Rome as elsewhere an apostle who was associated with a

63. "The Foundation of the Synoptic Tradition: (2) The Gospel of Mark", *BJRL* 28 (1944), pp. 119–136 (especially p. 131), reprinted in *Studies in the Gospels and Epistles* (Manchester, 1962), pp. 38–45 (especially p. 40).

64. Cf. C. H. Dodd, *About the Gospels* (Cambridge, 1950), pp. 1 f.; F. F. Bruce, "The Date and Character of Mark", in *Jesus and the Politics of his Day*, ed. E. Bammel (Cambridge, forthcoming).

65. *Petrus und Paulus in Rom* (Berlin, ²1927), p. 238.

66. Irenaeus, *Against Heresies* 3.3.1–3; for Hegesippus see Eusebius, *Hist. Eccl.* 4.22.3.

church in its early days was inevitably claimed as its founder.

Constantine's erection of the basilica of St. Peter on the Vatican hill was based on the belief that Peter's body was buried there – a belief going back at least to A.D. 180, when the Roman presbyter Gaius said that he could point out Peter's "trophy" or funerary monument on the Vatican hill.[67] The actual monument to which Gaius refers may well have been discovered in the course of excavations beneath St. Peter's in 1941 – a simple *aedicula* comprising three niches, in relation to which Constantine appears to have orientated the basilica. If (as seems likely) the monument is of the same date as a small water-channel in its immediate vicinity, it can be assigned to the time of Marcus Aurelius, whose name is stamped on several bricks of the channel – perhaps before his accession to the principate in A.D. 161, since he is designated Caesar, not Augustus.[68]

The rival site for Peter's burial (along with Paul) near the Memoria Apostolorum ad Catacumbas, on the Appian Way, must not pass unnoticed.[69] We cannot here discuss the respective claims of the two sites, but even in their rivalry they do together confirm the antiquity of the tradition of Peter's death and burial in Rome.

67. Eusebius, *Hist. Eccl.* 3.25.7.
68. Cf. J. M. C. Toynbee and J. B. Ward-Perkins, *The Shrine of St. Peter and the Vatican Excavations* (London, 1956); E. Kirschbaum, *The Tombs of St. Peter and St. Paul*, E. T. (London, 1959); G. F. Snyder, "Survey and 'New' Thesis on the Bones of Peter", *The Biblical Archaeologist* 32 (1969), pp. 2–24.
69. See H. Chadwick, "St. Peter and St. Paul in Rome: The Problem of the Memoria Apostolorum ad Catacumbas", *JTS* n.s. 8 (1957), pp. 31–52.

9. *"On this rock"*

When Peter was hailed as "The Rock", it was not quite certain which kind of rock he would prove to be. There is an oracle in the book of Isaiah which suggests that one and the same rock may provide a firm refuge in time of flood and become "a stone of offence and a rock of stumbling" to those who are swept against it (Isa. 8:14). So, in one and the same context, the first evangelist represents Jesus as saying to Peter, "on this rock I will build my church" and "you are an obstacle (*skandalon*) in my path" (Matt. 16:18, 23). Peter had it in him to be a stone of stumbling or to be a foundation stone.[70] Thanks to the intercession which his Master made for him in a critical hour, he strengthened his brethren and became a rock of stability and a focus of unity.

70. Cf. O. Cullmann, "L'apôtre Pierre instrument du diable et instrument de Dieu; la place de Matt. 16:16–19 dans la tradition primitive", in *New Testament Essays . . . in memory of T. W. Manson*, ed. A. J. B. Higgins (Manchester, 1959), pp. 94–105.

CHAPTER 2

STEPHEN AND OTHER HELLENISTS

1. Hellenists in the Jerusalem church

Almost from the earliest days of the Christian
community, it comprised two groups, described by
Luke as Hebrews and Hellenists. He introduces them
abruptly in Acts 6:1, without explaining who they
were: perhaps he takes it for granted that his readers
will be familiar with the terms. It is plain that in
the section of his narrative beginning with Acts 6:1
Luke is drawing on a fresh source; he moves from
the preceding section to this by means of a
transitional formula: "Now in these days when the
disciples were increasing. . . ." He may therefore be
reproducing the terminology of his source.

The Hebrews and Hellenists in the Jerusalem
church, says Luke, began to quarrel over the daily
distribution that was made to their widows (and
other needy persons) from the common fund.
Accordingly, at the instance of the apostles, seven
men were appointed to take charge of the distribution and see fair play – *septem uiri mensis ordinandis*[1],

1. So they are called in idiomatic Latin by W. M. Ramsay, *St. Paul the
Traveller and the Roman Citizen* (London, [14]1920), p. 375.

of whom Stephen was one. But it is clear that this was not their only rôle – perhaps not even their most important rôle. Their names are all Greek[2], and they were probably leaders of the Hellenistic group in the church. This group was foremost in propagating the Christian message throughout Judaea and the neighbouring regions; it eventually launched the Gentile mission, and in particular was responsible for founding the church of Syrian Antioch. The Hellenistic source which Luke follows in Acts 6, 7 and 8[3], and takes up again in Acts 11:19, may well have been an Antiochene source.

But who were these Hellenists?

The term is most probably to be understood in a cultural and especially in a linguistic sense: that is to say, Hellenists were Greek-speaking Jews. The Jews of Antioch and Alexandria and other parts of the western diaspora had been Greek-speaking for generations;[4] not only so, the presence of Greek-speaking Jews in Palestine itself, as early as the reign of the second Ptolemy (285–246 B.C.), is attested in the Zenon papyri.[5]

In Palestine many Jews would be bilingual, speaking both Aramaic and Greek. What then determined whether a Jew was designated a Hebrew or a Hellenist? C. F. D. Moule has suggested that the

2. Too much should not be built on this: two members of the twelve had Greek names (Andrew and Philip).

3. It has been held that Acts 8:14–24 comes from a Jerusalem source, with verse 25 serving as an editorial transition to the resumption of the Hellenistic source; cf. A. Ehrhardt, *The Acts of the Apostles* (Manchester, 1969), pp. 45–47.

4. Cf. M. Hengel, *Judaism and Hellenism*, E. T. (London, 1974).

5. Zenon, steward of Ptolemy's finance minister Apollonius, made an extensive journey through Palestine and Phoenicia on his master's behalf in 260–258 B.C.; cf. M. Rostovtzeff, *A Large Estate in Egypt in the Third Century B.C.* (Madison, 1922).

Hellenists were Jews who spoke Greek only; the Hebrews would be Jews who either spoke Aramaic only or (like Paul and many others) spoke both Aramaic and Greek.[6] (In the New Testament "Hebrew" is used in a linguistic sense to include Aramaic.)[7] Perhaps the decisive criterion was membership of a synagogue where the service was conducted in Hebrew or of one in which the scriptures were read, the prayers and blessings recited, and the sermon preached, in Greek. Such a synagogue would be the one in Jerusalem described in Acts 6:9 as the "Synagogue of the Freedmen – both Cyrenians and Alexandrians and those from Cilicia and Asia".[8] This was the synagogue attended by Stephen, whose interventions there sounded so subversive that they led to his conviction before the supreme court on a charge of blasphemy and to the dispersal of his fellow-Hellenists who were believed to share his views.

Stephen and Philip are the only two of the seven Hellenistic almoners of whom we have some detailed knowledge. Nicolas, the proselyte of Antioch,[9] is said by Irenaeus to have been the eponymous founder and teacher of the Nicolaitans,[10] who are condemned in two of the seven letters of the

6. C. F. D. Moule, "Once More, Who Were the Hellenists?" *The Expository Times* 70 (1958–59), pp. 100–102. This would cover Paul's designation of himself as a Hebrew (2 Cor. 11:22; Phil. 3:5).

7. It is used of Aramaic words in John 19:13, 17.

8. It is difficult to be sure how many synagogues are meant here – whether one or more.

9. Since Nicolas is explicitly called a proselyte, it may be assumed that the other six were Jews by birth. The fact that he is the only one of the seven whose native place is mentioned has been thought to reflect the author's special interest in Antioch; cf. J. Smith, *The Voyage and Shipwreck of St. Paul* (London, [4]1880), p. 4.

10. Irenaeus, *Against Heresies* 1.23 (ed. W. W. Harvey i, p. 214).

Apocalypse for permitting or practising "fornication" and the eating of idolatrous meat (Rev. 2:6, 15). These otherwise unknown Nicolaitans may have been antinomian libertines, or they may simply have declined to be subject to the Jerusalem decree of Acts 15:28f.[11] In the latter case, they could indeed have been called after the Nicolas of Acts 6:5, for a detachment from traditional Jewish law and custom seems to have characterized the group to which he belonged.[12]

2. *Stephen and his teaching*

In the Hellenistic synagogue which he attended in Jerusalem, Stephen propounded an interpretation of the Way much more radical than that maintained and taught by the twelve, especially with regard to the temple and all that it stood for. A public debate was arranged in which Stephen defended his position with powerful arguments. But, powerful as his arguments were, they appeared to threaten the sanctity of the temple as well as the permanent validity of the whole ancestral law of Israel. The coming of Jesus, Stephen maintained, involved the abrogation of the Mosaic customs and the cessation of sacrificial worship. This was construed as blasphemy against Moses and against God himself, and on this grave charge Stephen was arraigned before the Sanhedrin.

When Judaea became a Roman province in A.D. 6, capital jurisdiction was reserved to the Roman

11. See pp. 38, 91 ff.
12. Prochorus, another of the seven, is named in the fifth-century *Acts of John* as the author of that work and a disciple of the apostle-evangelist-divine.

governor;[13] in one area, however – offences against
the sanctity of the temple (whether by action or by
word) – the Sanhedrin was allowed to pronounce
and execute the death sentence.[14] It may be recalled
that, when Jesus was brought before the same court,
an attempt was made to convict him on a charge of
speaking against the temple: "I will destroy this
temple that is made with hands . . ." (Mark 14:57f.).
This episode from Mark's account of the trial of
Jesus is not reproduced by Luke; Luke has a habit
of omitting from his gospel motifs which he proposes
to develop in Acts.

Had this attempt to convict Jesus succeeded, it
would presumably have been unnecessary to refer
his case to Pilate. As it was, the attempt failed; but
the prosecution of Stephen on what was essentially
the same charge was more successful. It could not
well have been otherwise. When the accusation was
stated – "we have heard him say that this Jesus of
Nazareth will destroy this place [the temple] and
change the customs which Moses delivered to us"
(Acts 6:14) – and Stephen was invited to reply, his
reply took the form of a detailed restatement of the
arguments which had led to his arraignment.

Stephen's reply is not an epitome of Luke's own
position: Luke, in both parts of his work, reveals a
much more positive attitude to the temple than
Stephen does.[15]

13. Cf. Josephus, *BJ* 2.117: Coponius, first Roman prefect of Judaea,
received authority μέχρι τοῦ κτείνειν.

14. Cf. Josephus, *BJ* 6.124–126.

15. Luke's Gospel begins (1:8–23) and ends (24:53) in the temple; in
Acts not only do the apostles and their associates attend temple worship
(2:46; 3:1; 5:12) but Paul has a vision of Christ there (22:17–21) and
participates in a Nazirite ceremony there (21:26–30).

Stephen's argument takes the form of a retrospect of the history of the people of God. Throughout their history, the divine presence was never confined to one spot or even to one country: God revealed himself to Abraham in Mesopotamia, was with Joseph in Egypt, gave "living oracles" to Moses in the wilderness of Sinai (Acts 7:2, 9, 38). The nation of Israel had always shown hostility to God's messengers – to Joseph, to Moses, to the prophets, and most recently to "the Righteous One"[16] whose coming the prophets had foretold (Acts 7:52). The charge of blasphemy against Moses and against God came ill from the descendants of those who during the wilderness wanderings repudiated the leadership of Moses and abandoned the worship of the true God for idolatry.

As for the temple, Stephen implies that a fixed building of stone was no suitable shrine for a pilgrim people, as Israel was intended to be. The movable tabernacle of wilderness days was much more suitable; indeed, everything necessary for pure worship was available to the people in the wilderness, before ever they entered the holy land. Even when they did enter the land, the "tent of witness", made according to divine pattern,[17] continued to serve their requirements in worshipping the God of their fathers until "Solomon built a house for him" (Acts 7:44-47). Solomon's action is deprecated: "the Most High does not dwell in houses made with hands" (Acts 7:48). Therefore, to announce the supersession or destruction of the temple was not to commit blasphemy or

16. The same title occurs on the lips of Ananias of Damascus (Acts 22:14).
17. See p. 82.

sacrilege against God, because God was independent of any temple.

Stephen's arguments were not accepted; his "defence" served only to confirm the charges brought against him and so, in accordance with the Jewish law against blasphemy, he was executed by stoning.[18] We meet nothing quite so radical elsewhere in the New Testament. It was common ground to most of the early Christians (for which indeed they could adduce words of Jesus as a precedent)[19] that the temple-order had now been superseded by something better – a spiritual temple with spiritual priesthood and spiritual sacrifices[20] – but the idea that the temple was a mistake from the beginning is unparalleled in the New Testament. The nearest we come to Stephen's approach, so far as the New Testament writings are concerned, is in the Letter to the Hebrews; but the writer to the Hebrews simply ignores the temple and draws his analogies from the literary description of the wilderness tabernacle and its services.[21]

Attempts have been made to find analogies to Stephen's position among the Samaritans,[22] the Qumran community,[23] or the Ebionites.[24] The Samaritans,

18. Lev. 24:16; cf. Deut. 17:7.
19. Cf. Matt. 12:6; John 2:19.
20. Cf. Rom.12:1; Heb. 13:15f.; 1 Pet. 2:5.
21. See pp. 82 f.
22. Cf. A. Spiro and C. S. Mann's appendices in J. Munck, *The Acts of the Apostles*, Anchor Bible (Garden City, N.Y., 1967), pp. 285–304; M. H. Scharlemann, *Stephen: A Singular Saint* (Rome, 1968); C. H. H. Scobie, "The Origins and Development of Samaritan Christianity", *NTS* 19 (1972–73), pp. 390–414.
23. Cf. O. Cullmann, "The Significance of the Qumran Texts for Research into the Beginnings of Christianity", *JBL* 74 (1955), pp. 213–226, reprinted in *The Scrolls and the New Testament*, ed. K. Stendahl (London, 1958), pp. 18–32.

however, were not against the temple in principle:
they objected to the Jerusalem temple because they
believed that the holy hill of Gerizim was the
divinely-appointed location for the sanctuary of the
God of Israel.[25] The men of Qumran avoided the
Jerusalem temple while it was dominated by a high-
priesthood which they believed to be illegitimate; but
they looked forward to the resumption of acceptable
sacrifices in a purified temple under a worthy
priesthood – even if, for the time being, their own
community served as a spiritual sanctuary with its
inner council as the holy of holies.[26] The Ebionites'
negative attitude to the temple was probably a
rationalization of its overthrow in A.D. 70; James
the Just, whose memory they revered, had been
assiduous in his attendance at the temple during his
lifetime in the days when it was still standing.[27]

It is best to regard Stephen's speech as a manifesto
of the group in which he was a leader – a group of
Hellenists who were distinguished from other Hellenistic Jews by their belief in Jesus as Messiah or
Son of God, and who were at the same time
distinguished from other believers in Jesus by their
radical stance in relation to the ancestral customs
and the temple cult. This radical stance, for which
precedent could be found in some of the great
prophets of Israel, did not disappear with Stephen's
death: we shall recognize a later witness to it in a

24. Cf. H. J. Schoeps, *Theologie und Geschichte des Judenchristentums*
(Tübingen, 1949), pp. 440–445.

25. Cf. John 4:20.

26. 1QS 8.4–10. The restoration of priesthood and sacrifice is presup-
posed in 1QM 2.1–6. Cf. B. Gärtner, *The Temple and the Community in
Qumran and the New Testament* (Cambridge, 1965); also R. J. McKelvey,
The New Temple (Oxford, 1969).

27. See pp. 114 ff.

document of Alexandrian Christianity – the Letter of Barnabas.[28]

If those who maintained this radical stance were called Hellenists by their more conservative brethren, the word, in the sense of "Hellenizers", with an implication of disparagement (as Marcel Simon has suggested),[29] could have had a theological, as well as a cultural and linguistic, nuance.

Rudolf Bultmann, holding that the primitive kerygma was mediated to Paul through congregations of Hellenistic Christians, devoted the third chapter of his *Theology of the New Testament* (running to over a hundred pages) to a discussion of the kerygma of Hellenistic Christianity, in all its variety, by way of a preamble to his full exposition of Paul's theology (this by contrast with a mere thirty pages devoted to the message of Jesus).[30] If there were in fact as much information available about pre-Pauline Hellenistic Christianity as the space given to it by Bultmann might suggest, we should congratulate ourselves; I fear, however, that T. W. Manson was right in describing those hundred pages and more as "occupied with an imaginary account of the theology of the anonymous and otherwise unknown 'Hellenistic Communities'."[31]

3. The Hellenistic dispersion

Stephen's execution, according to Luke, was the

28. See pp. 62–64.
29. M. Simon, "St. Stephen and the Jerusalem Temple", *Journal of Ecclesiastical History* 2 (1951), pp. 127–142; cf. his *St. Stephen and the Hellenists in the Jerusalem Church* (London, 1958), pp. 12–18.
30. R. Bultmann, *Theology of the New Testament*, E. T., i (London, 1952), pp. 63–183.
31. T. W. Manson, *Studies in the Gospels and Epistles* (Manchester, 1962), p. 7.

signal for a campaign of repression against the
disciples of Jesus in Jerusalem and Judaea. A careful
study of Luke's record suggests that the Hellenists
were singled out for more concentrated attack – not
surprisingly, for regular temple-attenders like the
twelve and their followers would not be closely
associated in the public mind with an anti-temple
party. If, at the same time, those Hellenists preached
a law-free form of gospel, that would render them
the more obnoxious to defenders of the law of
Moses. The twelve and their followers (not to speak
of those who in a few years' time were to find their
natural leader in James the Just) might well have
been anxious to distance themselves from such a
subversive group.

One result of the campaign of repression was that
the church of Jerusalem became predominantly
"Hebrew" in composition, with a few exceptions like
Barnabas the Cypriot and another man of Cyprus,
Mnason by name, who was a foundation-member of
the Jerusalem church and was still resident there
nearly a quarter of a century later (Acts 21:16).
Another, and even more important, result was that
the dispersed Hellenists propagated the gospel much
farther afield – north as far as Antioch and probably
south and south-west as far as Alexandria and
Cyrenaica.

Philip, who was now evidently leader of the seven
in succession to Stephen, launched a mission in
Samaria. The Hellenists and the Samaritans are not
be equated with each other, but Philip's preaching
proved attractive to many of his Samaritan hearers.
He even attached to himself the Samaritan guru
Simon – Simon Magus of Christian tradition –

presumably with his followers.

Arnold Ehrhardt went so far as to find in the record of Simon's attachment to Philip (Acts 8:12f.) evidence for the incorporation of a pre-Christian gnostic sect into the fellowship of the gospel.[32] To be sure, Dr. Ehrhardt thought Philip's gospel was defective by Jerusalem standards, in that it did not teach the reception of the Holy Spirit in baptism. This was an inference from the fact that, although Philip's Samaritan converts, including Simon, had been "baptized into the name of the Lord Jesus" (Acts 8:16), they did not receive the Spirit until Peter and John, representatives of the twelve, came from Jerusalem and laid hands on them.[33] But it is not really implied by Luke that the preaching of Philip, or of the seven in general, was defective in the way that Dr. Ehrhardt thought. Luke, at any rate, looks on all seven as Spirit-filled men, Stephen outstandingly so (Acts 6:3, 5).

As for Simon Magus, while he had no difficulty in adhering to Philip, he was repudiated by Peter and John, and by the apostolic succession of later generations. In later Christian literature he figures as the father of all heresies and as a thorn in the sides of the apostles, especially of Peter. What precisely was the nature of Simon's teaching, which attracted the host of devotees who acclaimed in him "the power of God which is called Great" – or possibly "the revealer of divine power"[34] – is difficult to say.

---

32. A Ehrhardt, *The Framework of the New Testament Stories* (Manchester, 1964), p. 163; cf. E. Haenchen, *The Acts of the Apostles*, E. T. (Oxford, 1971), p. 307.

33. A preferable account of this delay is given by G. W. H. Lampe, *The Seal of the Spirit* (London, 1951), p. 72.

34. A. Klostermann took μεγάλη, "great", to be a transliteration of

He does at least seem to have taught "a syncretistic
scheme with a few Christian elements grafted on"[35]
– a form of incipient gnosticism, it might be said. It
appears, however, that the preaching of Philip (and,
we may suppose, of some of his fellow-Hellenists)
was more comprehensive than that of the twelve.
Primitive Christianity was more variegated than is
commonly recognized.

Philip, in Luke's narrative, moved from Samaria
to the neighbourhood of Gaza, where he effectively
"preached Jesus" to a God-fearing official from
Meroe in Nubia, who was on his way home from
a pilgrimage to Jerusalem (Acts 8:26–39). He then
turned north along the coastal road until he came to
Caesarea (Acts 8:40), and there we find him twenty
years later with his four prophesying daughters (Acts
21:8f.). Caesarea now appears as the main Judaean
centre of Hellenistic Christianity, at least until the
troubles of A.D. 66, when some of the leading
Caesarean Christians emigrated to the province of
Asia.[36]

4. The church of Antioch

Luke's Antiochene source then turns its attention
to Syrian Antioch, evangelized by unnamed refugees
from the persecution in Judaea that followed
Stephen's death. According to Luke, when they first
came to Antioch they preached only to their fellow-

Hebrew or Aramaic *megalle(h)*, "revealer", the phrase "which is called"
being then a typical Lukan apology for the use of a foreign term
(*Probleme im Aposteltexte* [Gotha, 1883], pp. 15ff.).

35. R. McL. Wilson, *The Gnostic Problem* (London, 1958), p. 100.

36. See p. 121.

Hellenists – Greek-speaking Jews like themselves – but some of them, whose roots were in Cyprus and Cyrene, began to tell the story to Greek-speaking pagans as well.[37] This was the commencement of a large-scale mission to Gentiles. The development in Antioch may well have been paralleled in other places, of which we have no comparable record.

In Antioch, however, several strands of primitive Christianity met. Barnabas the Cypriot, who enjoyed the confidence of the Jerusalem leaders, was sent by them to superintend and direct the Christian advance in Antioch; he was shortly afterwards joined by Paul, from Tarsus, and later Peter also visited Antioch. Antioch thus became a centre from which various understandings of Christianity radiated in a number of directions through the Gentile world. C. K. Barrett has drawn attention to at least three strands of Gentile Christianity which Acts helps us to distinguish: one which runs back to Stephen and his Hellenistic colleagues, one which looked to Peter for its leadership, and of course "the radical (or, better, converted conservative) mission of Paul himself". When, with the fall of Jerusalem in A.D. 70, "Gentile Christianity had in a new way to stand on its own feet", it was necessary for the competing groups "to come to terms with one another"; and Acts, Professor Barrett holds, can best be understood as "a monument of this process".[38] At present it is

37. In many manuscripts of Acts 11:20 these are called Hellenists ('Ελληνιστάς) rather than Hellenes or Greeks ("Ελληνας), but the context makes it plain that Gentiles are intended.

38. C. K. Barrett, "Acts and the Pauline Corpus", *The Expository Times* 88 (1976–77), pp. 4f.; cf. F. Hahn, *Mission in the New Testament*, E. T. (London, 1965); S. G. Wilson, *The Gentiles and the Gentile Mission in Luke-Acts* (Cambridge, 1973).

important to note that all three of these strands were represented at an early date in Antioch.

5. *The Letter of "Barnabas"*

What happened in Antioch no doubt happened, to a greater or less degree, in Egyptian Alexandria, but the historical beginnings of Alexandrian Christianity are, unfortunately, almost completely undocumented. Alexandria, from its foundation in 331 B.C., was not only the main centre of Hellenistic culture but also the home of the most illustrious community of dispersion Jews. By the end of the second century A.D. it was the seat of the most outstanding intellectual movement in the Christian world. But on the setting in which this movement received its first impetus we are scantily informed.

The New Testament canon probably includes one Alexandrian document if, as I believe, the Letter to the Hebrews was sent by an Alexandrian Christian to a Hellenistic house-church in Rome. It is certainly a document of *Hellenistic* Christianity in the general tradition of Stephen and his associates, although (as has been said above) its position with regard to the temple is different from Stephen's. We shall come back to the Letter to the Hebrews.[39]

For the present we turn to another document of Hellenistic Christianity which does reproduce Stephen's radical rejection of the temple cult. This is the Letter of Barnabas, which hovered for a time on the brink of the New Testament canon but, fortunately, did not succeed in establishing a place within

39. See pp. 79 ff.

it. It is to be dated later in the first or early in the second century. While it includes features which are not characteristically Alexandrian, it is most probably to be assigned to an Alexandrian author.[40]

This author deplores the attitude of those who pin their hopes to the material sanctuary and not rather to God their Creator (16:1). Among scriptural *testimonia* which he quotes in support of his argument he lays special weight on one which Stephen also quotes (Acts 7:49f.) – the opening words of Isa. 66:

> Heaven is my throne
> and the earth is my footstool;
> what is the house which you would build for me,
> and what is the place of my rest?

Even more pointed is his tracing the record of Israel's idolatry back to the wilderness wanderings and the worship of the golden calf. Moses, he says, came down from Mount Sinai with the divine law-code in his hands to give to the people, but when he saw their idolatry he broke the stone tablets in pieces. "Moses received the law, but they were not worthy" (14:1–4; cf.4:8). Referring to the same incident, Stephen says that it was then that "God turned and gave them over to worship the host of heaven" (Acts 7:42), and he applies in this sense the rhetorical question of Amos 5:25: "Did you bring to me sacrifices and offerings the forty years in the wilderness, O house of Israel?" The answer implied by Stephen is: "No, not to me, but to Moloch and

40. Cf. R. A. Kraft, *The Apostolic Fathers, 3; Barnabas and the Didache* (New York, 1965), pp. 45–48; C. H. Roberts, *Manuscript, Society and Belief in Early Christian Egypt* (London, 1979), p. 36.

other false gods." To the same effect the Letter of
Barnabas (2:4–8) quotes two other rhetorical questions
from the prophets: "What is the multitude of your
sacrifices to me? . . ." (Isa. 1:11) and "Did I
command your fathers in the day they left Egypt to
bring me burnt offerings and sacrifices? . . ." (Jer.
7:22). According to Hebrews the sacrificial order was
instituted "until the time of reformation" (Heb. 9:10)
– that is, until Christ came to accomplish his perfect
work. But according to the Letter of Barnabas, it
was not divinely instituted at all; it was a misun-
derstanding and perversion of the true (allegorical)
teaching of the Pentateuchal law, which the church
accepts and practises. The sacrificial ritual as carried
out by the Jews is a token of their blindness and
disobedience, "from Egypt even until now." The
divine covenant which Israel repudiated in Moses'
day has been transferred in its real, spiritual sense
to Christians.

The supersession of Israel by the church is a
commonplace in early Christian writers, but few
asserted so emphatically that even in the pre-
Christian era Israel's ritual law lacked so much as a
token validity. The affinities between Barnabas and
Stephen might be explained in terms of Barnabas's
dependence on Acts, or the dependence of Barnabas
and Stephen (or Luke) on a common collection of
Old Testament *testimonia;* but it is best to explain
them in terms of a particularly radical Hellenistic
tradition which stems from Stephen and his circle
and found a home in early Alexandrian Christianity.[41]

41. Cf. L. W. Barnard, "St. Stephen and Early Alexandrian Christianity", *NTS* 7 (1960–61), pp. 31–45.

6. Apollos of Alexandria

We meet one outstanding Alexandrian Christian in the New Testament in the person of Apollos, a Jew of Alexandria who, when he first appears, has learned the story of Jesus and argues from the Old Testament writings that Jesus is the Messiah.

Our earliest literary references to Apollos are found in Paul's first letter to the Corinthian church, written in the spring of A.D. 55. From these references we gather that, some time after the end of Paul's eighteen-months residence in Corinth, during which he had planted and fostered the church in that city, Apollos came and continued the work which Paul had begun. "I planted", says Paul, "Apollos watered, but God gave the growth" (1 Cor. 3:6). Paul betrays no hint of disapproval of Apollos or his work: in his estimation, Apollos and he were "fellow workers for God" (1 Cor. 3:9), each performing his divinely appointed task.

Nevertheless, some members of the church in Corinth, not content to accept both Paul and Apollos as servants of God through both of whom they had received heavenly grace, tried to claim the one and the other as party leaders. "I belong to Paul", said one group; "I belong to Apollos", said another (1 Cor. 1:12). As we have already, yet another group claimed to belong to "Kephas" (Peter).[42]

A good part of the first section of 1 Corinthians (chapters 1–4) is devoted to a polemic against this manifestation of party spirit, and in this polemic Paul makes free use of the names of Apollos and

42. See p. 40.

himself to illustrate his argument. He was careful
not to refer to Peter more than was necessary
(relations between himself and the leader of the
twelve had been delicate ever since their public
confrontation at Antioch);[43] but there was sufficient
mutual confidence between himself and Apollos for
him to use their two names by way of example for
his converts' benefit, "that none of you may be
puffed up in favour of one against another" (1 Cor.
4:6).

This mutual confidence comes to expression again
towards the end of the letter, where Paul says, "As
for our brother Apollos, I strongly urged him to
visit you with the other brethren, but it was plainly
not God's will for him to come now; he will come
when he has opportunity" (1 Cor. 16:12). The details
of this postponed visit are obscure to us; in fact, we
cannot be quite sure whether it was God's will or
his own will that stood in the way of Apollos going
to Corinth just then,[44] but some recent contact
between Paul and Apollos in Ephesus (from which
Paul wrote) is implied. Although Paul was not too
happy about some Christian visitors who came to
Corinth and tried to build on the foundation which
he had laid, he clearly had no misgivings about a
visit by Apollos.

The next literary reference to Apollos comes in
Acts 18:24 – 19:1; it supplies just the background
that is necessary for us to read Paul's allusions to

43. See p. 34.
44. The Greek text says οὐκ ἦν θέλημα, literally "it was not will" (cf.
the absolute use of θέλημα for God's will in 1 Macc. 3:60; Rom. 2:18).
Apollos had evidently returned from Corinth to Ephesus; perhaps he
was embarrassed by being set up as a party leader at Corinth in rivalry
to Paul.

him in 1 Corinthians with greater understanding.
After Paul had completed his evangelization of
Corinth, says Luke, and had set sail for Palestine,
leaving his friends Priscilla and Aquila in Ephesus
(where he had made a brief stop on his journey):

> A Jew named Apollos, a native of Alexandria, arrived
> in Ephesus. He was a man of culture, with a mastery
> of the scriptures. He had been instructed in the way
> of the Lord, and with fervour of spirit he told the
> story of Jesus and taught it accurately, although he
> knew no baptism but John's. He began to speak openly
> in the synagogue, and when Priscilla and Aquila heard
> him they took him home and set forth the way of God
> to him more accurately. When he wished to cross over
> into Achaia the brethren [in Ephesus] encouraged him
> and wrote to the disciples to give him a welcome.
> When he arrived [in Corinth] he gave the believers
> great help through the grace [bestowed on him], for he
> powerfully confuted the Jews by his public demonstra-
> tion from the scriptures that the Christ [i.e. the Messiah
> of whom the scriptures spoke] was Jesus.

In the Western text of this passage Apollos is called
Apollonius (no doubt the full name of which Apollos
is an abridgement), and he is said to have received
his instruction in the way of the Lord "in his home
city (*patris*)", that is, in Alexandria. This implies that
Christianity had reached Alexandria by about A.D.
50, and this is highly probable, no matter how much
or little evidence was available to the Western
editor.[45]

45. Apollos's going from Ephesus to Corinth is expanded thus in the
Western text: "Some Corinthians who were visiting Ephesus and heard
him begged him to cross over with them to their home city (πατρίς).

"A man of culture" is Moulton and Milligan's suggested rendering of *anēr logios*,[46] otherwise translated "a learned man" (RV, NIV) or "an eloquent man" (AV, RSV, NEB). Of these two translations the former corresponds to the sense of the adjective in classical Greek, but the latter agrees with its meaning in Hellenistic[47] and Modern Greek.

Apollos's "mastery of the scriptures" probably consisted both in his familiarity with the sacred text and in his skill in interpreting messianic prophecy in a Christian sense. Whether or not it also indicates his competence in the allegorical method practised by Philo and other Platonists of his native Alexandria we have no means of knowing.

Evidently some members of the Corinthian church were so greatly impressed by Apollos and his ministry that they enrolled themselves – theoretically, at any rate – as members of his school: "I belong to Apollos." What, we may ask, was there about Apollos's ministry that made it appeal to them more than Paul's? Possibly Apollos's eloquence was contrasted with Paul's unimpressive delivery,[48] or conceivably his more imaginative flights of exposition were preferred to Paul's deliberate eschewing of

---

When he consented, the Ephesians wrote to the disciples in Corinth to give the man a welcome. When he visited Achaia he was very helpful in the churches, for he powerfully confuted the Jews, publicly debating and demonstrating from the scriptures that Jesus was the Christ." This expansion is editorial, and a trifle awkward: if Corinthian Christians invited Apollos to go home with them, it should not have been necessary for the Ephesian disciples to send a letter of commendation to the Corinthian church.

46. J. H. Moulton and G. Milligan, *The Vocabulary of the Greek New Testament* (Edinburgh, 1930), p. 378.

47. Cf. Phrynichus, *Eclogae Nominum et Verborum Atticorum*, ed. C. A. Lobeck (Leipzig, 1820), p. 198.

48. Cf. 2 Cor. 10:10.

"lofty words or wisdom" among the Corinthians (1 Cor. 2:1). There does not appear to have been any difference of principle between the "Apollos" party and the "Paul" party; it was simply deplorable, from Paul's point of view, that such parties should be formed. "What then is Apollos? What is Paul? Servants through whom you believed, as the Lord assigned to each" (1 Cor. 3:5). In his references to Apollos, Paul shows no trace of the reserve which can be discerned not far below the surface when he speaks of Peter. Some members at least of the "Peter" party were disposed to question Paul's apostolic freedom, as the "Apollos" party was not.

In some measure the two accounts of Apollos complement each other. For example, if we had the account of Acts only, we should not know that Paul and Apollos ever met, whereas the evidence of 1 Corinthians makes it plain that they were personally acquainted and were on terms of mutual esteem and indeed affection.[49]

According to the record of Acts, Apollos, for all his accurate acquaintance with the story of Jesus, knew no baptism but that inaugurated by John the Baptist. How was this? That Apollos was not unique in this regard is indicated by the next paragraph in

49. Apollos is mentioned once again in the New Testament – in Tit. 3:13, where Paul charges Titus to "speed Zenas the lawyer and Apollos on their way" and to "see that they lack nothing". Our knowledge of the life-setting of this personal note is so minimal that we cannot determine where Apollos (with the otherwise unknown Zenas) had come from or where he was going. P. N. Harrison thought that the message of Tit. 3:12–15 was sent to Titus while he was at Corinth on the mission mentioned in 2 Cor. 7:5–16 (*The Problem of The Pastoral Epistles* [Oxford, 1921], pp. 115–118); cf. S. G. Wilson, *Luke and Pastoral Epistles* (London, 1979), pp. 127f. All that can be said is that Apollos is referred to, as before, in friendly terms.

Acts, where Paul meets twelve "disciples" at Ephesus who had been baptized, but only with John's baptism, and knew nothing of the Holy Spirit (Acts 19:1–7). When Luke uses the term "disciples" without qualification, as he does here, he regularly means disciples of Jesus, and that is probably the meaning in Acts 19:1. Luke does not suggest that there was any connexion between these twelve men and Apollos, and we cannot be sure whether there was or not.

Of Apollos himself, however, we may say that the gospel had reached him by a different route from that traced in the main course of Luke's narrative or from that presupposed in Paul's letters. For both Luke and Paul, baptism is "into the name of the Lord Jesus" (Acts 8:16; 19:5; cf. 1 Cor. 1:13 with Gal. 3:27; Rom. 6:3); for both Luke and Paul, the present age is the age of the Spirit. Paul had not been among those on whom the Spirit fell on the day of Pentecost: his conversion, baptism and reception of the Spirit took place in independence of the Jerusalem church. Yet he became, as Arnold Ehrhardt put it, "one of the greatest assets for the Church at Jerusalem",[50] for under his influence, when not by his personal action, versions of the gospel which were defective by Jerusalem standards were brought into line with the form of Christianity which he and the Jerusalem leaders held in common. The instruction of Apollos by Paul's friends Priscilla and Aquila, and Paul's administering Christian baptism to the twelve disciples at Ephesus, are examples of this.

50. *The Framework of the New Testament Stories* (Manchester, 1964), p. 94.

7. *The beginnings of Alexandrian Christianity*

When, after the martyrdom of Stephen, "those who were scattered went about preaching the word" (Acts 8:4), they probably went south-west from Judaea as well as north. We have more information about those who travelled through Phoenicia and reached Antioch, but if men of Cyrene were among those who preached the gospel in Antioch, it is likely that other men of Cyrene preached the same gospel nearer to their own home territory. The gospel would have penetrated the Jewish community of Alexandria about the same time as it reached Antioch.

Could Apollos have derived his knowledge of the Way from such a Hellenistic mission? One difficulty about supposing that he could is the fact that Luke nowhere suggests that the gospel preached by these Hellenists was defective in the way that Apollos's knowledge of it was. Despite Arnold Ehrhardt's suspicion that Philip's preaching lacked the emphasis on the gift of the Spirit that characterized the full-orbed apostolic message, an evangelist whose converts were "baptized into the name of the Lord Jesus" (Acts 8:16)[51] cannot be made responsible for a version of Christianity which knew only the baptism of John. It may be, of course, that not all the Hellenistic preachers were so well informed as Stephen and Philip were; but on this possibility we can but speculate.

Some scholars have found evidence for the arrival of Christianity in Alexandria in a letter sent by the Emperor Claudius to the people of that city in the

51. See p. 59.

first year of his principate (A.D. 41), a papyrus copy
of which was acquired by the British Museum in
1921.[52] There had recently been outbreaks of civil
strife between the Greek and Jewish communities of
Alexandria, and it is principally with this strife that
the letter is concerned. Claudius addresses first the
Greeks and then the Jews, bidding them live at
peace with one another, and with regard to the
latter he says (lines 88–99):

> I bid the Jews for their part not to agitate for more
> than they have previously enjoyed, and never again to
> send two embassies, as though they lived in two
> separate cities – the like of which has never happened
> before. Moreover, they must not bring in or invite Jews
> who sail in from Syria or down from [other parts of]
> Egypt; this is the sort of thing which will compel me
> to redouble my suspicions. Otherwise I will proceed
> against them with the utmost severity for fomenting a
> general plague which infests the whole world.

The "general plague which infests the whole world"
is probably militant Jewish messianism, which was
rife during Claudius's principate not only in Judaea
but in many cities throughout the Roman Empire.
Claudius had to expel Jews from Rome about A.D.
49 because of their riotous conduct "at the instigation
of Chrestus" *(impulsore Chresto),*[53] and when Paul
and his fellow-missionaries came to Thessalonica
about the same time it was easy for their opponents

52. P. Lond. 1912. *Editio princeps* in H. I. Bell, *Jews and Christians in
Egypt* (London, 1924), pp. 1–37; cf. E. M. Smallwood, *Documents
illustrating the Principates of Gaius, Claudius and Nero* (Cambridge, 1967),
No. 370, pp. 99–102.
53. Suetonius, *Claudius* 25.4

to stir up suspicion against them by classing them with "the men who have subverted the whole world" and charging them with "acting against the decrees of Caesar, saying that there is another king, Jesus" (Acts 17:6f.).

The Jews whose immigration into Alexandria from other parts of Egypt or from Syria was forbidden by Claudius were probably called in by the Alexandrian Jews to strengthen them against their hostile Greek neighbours. Attempts have indeed been made to see in his words (particularly with regard to incomers from Syria, which included Palestine) "the first secular reference to Christian missionaries".[54] But this is reading into the text something which it does not imply. The riots in the Jewish community of Rome "at the instigation of Chrestus" may indeed have been caused by the recent introduction of Christianity into that community, but the riots at Alexandria, which caused Claudius such concern, were not within the Jewish community but between it and the Greek community.

But what of the "two embassies" which made Claudius so indignant? (Possibly the embassies had come to Rome to congratulate him on his accession and had seized the opportunity to make interested representations to him.) The language points most naturally not to one embassy from the Greek community and one from the Jewish community, but to two from the Jewish community – rival embassies

54. E. M. Blaiklock, *Out of the Earth* (London, 1957), p. 37; cf. G. de Sanctis, "Claudio e i Giudei d'Alessandria", *Rivista di filologia* 52 (1924), pp. 473ff.; S. Reinach, "La première allusion au christianisme dans l'histoire", *Revue de l'histoire des religions* 90 (1924), pp. 108–122; H. J. Cadbury, *The Book of Acts in History* (New York/London, 1955), pp. 116f.

at that, "as though they lived in two separate cities". A split within the Jewish community is implied. It cannot be proved that this split was not due to the recent arrival of Jewish-Christian missionaries, who had persuaded a fair number of Alexandrian Jews of the truth of the gospel; but it was due much more probably to a visit from Judaean extremists, who had won some Alexandrian Jews over to a militant policy, while the others preferred a policy of conciliation with their Greek neighbours. In short, the letter of Claudius does not appear to throw any light on the beginnings of Alexandrian Christianity.

It has been widely held, especially under the influence of Walter Bauer,[55] that Alexandrian Christianity was gnostic from its inception, and that what later came to be recognized as orthodoxy did not gain the upper hand until well into the second half of the second century. Eusebius's story of the founding of the church of Alexandria by Mark[56] (which may have as its historical basis the introduction of the Gospel of Mark to Alexandria)[57] seems to reflect an attempt to provide Alexandrian Christianity with an orthodox and near-apostolic pedigree in association with Rome. The later regulative status of Roman Christianity might be thought to have been anticipated by Luke – if only inadvertently – when

55. W. Bauer, *Orthodoxy and Heresy in Early Christianity*, E. T. from 2nd German edition (Philadelphia, 1971), pp. 44–60. (The 1st German edition was published in 1934.) See p. 75, n.61.

56. Eusebius, *Hist. Eccl.* 2.16.

57. Cf. C. H. Roberts, "The Christian Book and the Greek Papyri", *JTS* 50 (1949), pp. 155–168; L. W. Barnard, "St. Mark and Alexandria", *HTR* 57 (1974), pp. 145–150. A variant of this tradition is reflected in the fragment of a letter by (probably) Clement of Alexandria first published in M. Smith, *Clement of Alexandria and a Secret Gospel of Mark* (Cambridge, Mass., 1973); cf. F. F. Bruce, *The "Secret" Gospel of Mark* (London, 1974).

he tells how the gaps in Apollos's knowledge of the Way were filled in by Priscilla and Aquila, perhaps founder-members of the Christian community in Rome, which they had been compelled to leave by Claudius's edict some three years before.

The strong Roman influence, however, does not belong to the earliest stages of Alexandrian Christianity.[58] The character of the "strong Jewish strain"[59] which has been detected in it bespeaks Palestinian influence in its earliest days.[60] Nor were those earliest days so completely marked by gnosticism as Walter Bauer maintained. Gnosticism did indeed find very fertile soil in Alexandria and elsewhere in Egypt. But C. H. Roberts' detailed study of early Christian papyri in Egypt, including especially their treatment of *nomina sacra*, has led to the conclusion that Bauer's theory is implausible.[61] Of fourteen Christian texts from Egypt that Dr. Roberts would date before A.D. 200, only one may reasonably be

58. H Lietzmann clearly exaggerates when he suggests that the Alexandrian church "was founded as a daughter church to Rome and endowed by Rome with episcopal authority" (*The Founding of the Church Universal*, E. T. [London, ²1950], p. 67).

59. C. H. Roberts, *Manuscript, Society and Belief in Early Christian Egypt* (London, 1979), p. 45.

60. W. D. Davies has gone so far as to suggest that the Jewish Christians who carried the faith from Palestine to Alexandria acknowledged the leadership of James ("Paul and Jewish Christianity according to Cardinal Daniélou", *Recherches de Science Religieuse* 60 [1972], pp. 69–79). The followers of James did exercise some influence in Egyptian Christianity (see p. 119, n.61), but Alexandrian Christianity is more likely to have been originally the fruit of Hellenistic outreach.

61. See his Schweich Lectures for 1977: *Manuscript, Society and Belief in Early Christian Egypt* (London, 1979); also his review of W. Bauer, *Rechtgläubigkeit und Ketzerei im ältesten Christentum* (Tübingen, ²1964), in *JTS* n.s. 16 (1965), pp. 183–185. Cf. too E. A. Judge and S. R. Pickering, "Papyrus Documentation of Church and Community in Egypt to the Mid-Fourth Century", *Jahrbuch für Antike und Christentum* 20 (1977), pp. 47–71.

regarded as gnostic.[62] There are persistent features
of church government in Alexandria which go back
to the time before there was a single, centrally
organized church in the city. But it may well be
that, about the middle of the second century, the
influential catechetical school of Alexandria fell under
gnostic domination and that this necessitated a
purge, with Roman aid, when Pantaenus became its
leader.

8. The Galilaean thesis

When Palestinian influence is mentioned, it need
not be Judaean; it may be Samaritan or Galilaean.
And it has been argued by a number of scholars
that the Galilaean contribution to early Christianity
has been overlooked: that, where early Christian
strands are recognized which appear not to be
traceable to Jerusalem or the Pauline mission, the
possibility of their Galilaean origin should be considered.[63] In particular, the "defective" theology of
Apollos or of the twelve disciples at Ephesus might
have stemmed from Galilee. There is no certainty
that it was in his native Alexandria that Apollos
became acquainted with the story of Jesus, despite
the Western gloss to this effect. He was evidently a
traveller – perhaps an itinerant merchant like that
Ananias who introduced Judaism to the royal house
of Adiabene[64] – and he could have met Christian
preachers in any one of a number of places which

62. *Manuscript, Society and Belief* . . ., p. 52.
63. The seminal exposition of this thesis is E. Lohmeyer, *Galiläa und
Jerusalem* (Göttingen, 1936).
64. Josephus, *Ant.* 20.41.

he visited. Might these preachers have come from Galilee?

The argument runs as follows. Jesus had more disciples in Galilee than in Jerusalem. Not all his Galilaean disciples came up to Jerusalem for the Passover which witnessed his passion, and the majority of those who did come up probably went back as soon as possible. The number of Galilaean disciples was considerably in excess of the hundred and twenty whom Luke enumerates in Jerusalem on the eve of Pentecost. We do not know where it was that Jesus appeared in resurrection "to more than five hundred brethren at one time" (1 Cor. 15:6), but the chances are that it was in Galilee rather than Judaea. No doubt the closing months of Jesus' Galilaean ministry saw a decline in his popularity, but a number of his followers there remained loyal, and their faith was confirmed when he appeared in resurrection in Galilee.

If they were not present in Jerusalem on the day of Pentecost they would presumably not have shared in the outpouring of the Spirit. As for being baptized in the name of Jesus as the three thousand Jerusalem converts were, they no more required this than did their fellow-Galilaeans the apostles. They were already disciples of Jesus, and did not need any evangelization or confirmation from Jerusalem, as did their Samaritan neighbours to the south. They could continue to proclaim the good news of the kingdom of God in the name of their crucified and risen Master, even if they knew no baptism but John's and had no clear understanding that the age of the Spirit had dawned.

If they sought a mission-field beyond the frontiers

of Galilee, Syria lay close at hand. Damascus in particular comes to mind. It figures in the narratives of Paul's conversion both in Galatians and in Acts. It was Paul's first missionary base, before ever he met the leaders of the Jerusalem church (Gal. 1:15–17). Luke seems to distinguish at Damascus between refugees from the persecution in Judaea, whom Paul set out to arrest and take back in chains to Jerusalem, and native Damascene disciples, like Ananias, "well spoken of by all the Jews who lived there" (Acts 22:12).[65]

If Ananias and other Damascenes had received the gospel before the persecution which broke out after Stephen's death, from whom did they receive it? May it not have been from Galilaean disciples?

The argument, unfortunately, has to be conducted in a vacuum – as may be seen from the way in which each stage of it is introduced by the word "if". After Jesus' departure from Galilee some months before his death we know absolutely nothing of how his cause fared in that region until, as Luke puts it in a transitional summary, the persecution which followed Stephen's death died down and "the church throughout all Judaea and Galilee and Samaria had peace" (Acts 9:31). The implication of this statement is that Galilee was one of the areas to which refugees from the persecution "went . . . preaching the word" (Acts 8:4).[66]

---

65. A possible indebtedness of Damascene Christianity to the Zadokite covenanters of Damascus (CD 6.5, 19; 7.19; 19.34; 20.12) is even more problematical than a possible indebtedness to Galilee.

66. For a brief but telling critique of the Galilaean thesis see G. B. Caird, *The Apostolic Age* (London, 1955), pp. 87–99.

9. The Letter to the Hebrews

The importance of Apollos in the New Testament would be greatly enhanced if he could be identified with the author of the anonymous Letter to the Hebrews. This identification is not an ancient proposal; it appears to have been put forward first by Martin Luther in a sermon on 1 Cor. 3:4ff. preached in 1537[67] and then in his commentary on Genesis (1545).[68] In his lectures on Hebrews in 1517–18 Luther had accepted the conventional Pauline ascription,[69] but in the preface to Hebrews in his German version of the New Testament (1522) he described the author as "an excellent man of learning, who had been a disciple of the apostles and learned much from them, and who was very well versed in scripture".[70] This description bears such a close resemblance to Luke's account of Apollos in Acts 18:24 that Luther may reasonably be supposed to have had Apollos in mind when he wrote his preface, though he had not yet sufficient confidence to name him.

Luther's identification of Apollos as the writer to the Hebrews was at least a brilliant guess, in which he has been followed by many commentators and others down to the present day. Ceslas Spicq, who himself adopts this identification, lists over forty others who have done so, from Théodore de Bèze in 1582 onwards, and his list could be augmented.[71]

67. *Luthers Werke*, Weimarer Ausgabe 45, p. 389.
68. *Luthers Werke*, Weimarer Ausgabe 44, p. 709.
69. *Luthers Werke*, Weimarer Ausgabe 57, Teil 3, pp. 1ff.; E. T. by J. Atkinson, *Luther: Early Theological Works* (London, 1962), pp. 19ff.
70. *Die deutsche Bibel*, Weimarer Ausgabe 7, p. 344.
71. C. Spicq, *L'épître aux Hébreux*, i (Paris, 1952), pp. 207–219. A more

The Alexandrian affinities of the outlook, style and vocabulary of the letter have been thought to speak in favour of Apollos's authorship. The writer seems not only to know such literary products of Alexandrian Judaism as Wisdom and 4 Maccabees, but also to have some acquaintance with the thought and language of Philo – without, however, sharing Philo's philosophical presuppositions or allegorical method.[72] That he himself was an Alexandrian is probable; that he was "a man of culture, with a mastery of the scriptures", is certain, as is also the fact that he knew the gospel story at second hand (Heb. 2:3). But all this does not dictate his identification with Apollos, unless we suppose that Apollos was the only person in the first Christian century answering to this description.

Faced with the problem of reviving the flagging faith of the Christians to whom he writes, he challenges them with a presentation of Jesus as the supreme and only effective mediator between God and man. This mediation was exercised primaevally in the creation of the world and is exercised continuously in its maintenance. Here, although the designation "Wisdom" is not applied to Jesus, Jesus is clearly viewed as personally embodying the *sophia* of the Jewish wisdom literature, not least of the Alexandrian Book of Wisdom. The description of

recent defender of the Apollos ascription is H. W. Montefiore, *The Epistle to the Hebrews* (London/New York, 1964), pp. 9–30; he suggests that Hebrews was sent by Apollos between A.D. 52 and 54 to a group of his friends at Corinth and identifies "those *from Italy*" (Heb. 13:24) with Priscilla and Aquila, described in Acts 18:2 as "newly come *from Italy*".

72. Cf. R. Williamson, *Philo and the Epistle to the Hebrews* (Leiden, 1970); R. H. Nash, "The Notion of Mediator in Alexandrian Judaism and the Epistle to the Hebrews", *Tyndale Bulletin* 30 (forthcoming).

Jesus as the "reflection" (*apaugasma*) of the glory of God and the "very stamp" of his essence (Heb. 1:3) echoes the description of Wisdom as "a reflection (*apaugasma*) of eternal light, . . . and an image" of the goodness of God (Wisd. 7:26).

Secondly, Jesus' mediation is exercised in his being the unique revealer in whom God has spoken his final and perfect word to mankind – this word being the gospel (Heb. 1:2a; 2:3).

Thirdly, Jesus' mediation is exercised in his self-offering to cleanse his people from inward sin and in his eternal priestly ministry, discharged in the heavenly sanctuary on the basis of that one self-offering.

The writer to the Hebrews is not a Philonist, although he shares Philo's intellectual background. Philo, when first introduced to the Platonic doctrine of ideas, was persuaded in a flash of mystical insight that this was eternal truth, and that all other truth – especially the truth of the Hebrew law and prophets, which he had inherited – must be understood and interpreted in Platonic terms. The writer to the Hebrews did not absorb Plato's doctrine into his system as Philo did. For him, the Jewish doctrine of the two ages is more basic than the doctrine of the upper and lower worlds. The hinge on which the two ages turn is the appearance of Christ on earth, where he suffered death as an atonement for his people's sin, once for all. His death is not the earthly realization of an eternal sacrifice; it requires neither continuation nor repetition. But on the strength of that one finished sacrifice Christ, now exalted, exercises a perpetual intercessory priesthood for his people.

One of the most pervasive Old Testament *testimonia* for the exaltation of Christ used in the early church is Ps. 110:1, where an oracle is communicated from the God of Israel to one whom the psalmist calls "my lord", with the invitation: "Sit at my right hand, till I make your enemies your footstool."[73] The writer to the Hebrews makes the fullest use of this oracle, emphasizing, for example, that Christ (unlike the continually standing priests of Aaron's line) is a *seated* priest because his sacrificial work has been completed once for all. But with this oracle he conjoins another, from verse 4 of the same psalm: "The LORD has sworn and will not change his mind, 'You are a priest for ever after the order of Melchizedek'." He was the first Christian thinker, so far as we know, to apply this oracle to Christ, and in it he finds scriptural authority for his presentation of Christ as his people's high priest.

The one point where the writer seems to draw on the Platonic/Philonic doctrine of the two worlds is in Heb. 8:2; 9:11, 23 f., where Israel's earthly sanctuary, with the ministry carried out in it, is portrayed as a material copy of the heavenly sanctuary where Christ carries out *his* ministry. But even for this he finds scriptural authority, in the passage where Moses, receiving instructions for the erection and equipment of the tabernacle in the wilderness, is commanded to make everything "according to the pattern" which God showed him on Mount Sinai (Exod. 25:9, 40). Moses' seeing of this "pattern" is understood as a vision of the

---

73. Cf. M. Gourgues, *A la droite de Dieu: Résurrection de Jésus et Actualisation du Psaume 110:1 dans le Nouveau Testament* (Paris, 1978).

spiritual sanctuary where Jesus is for ever enthroned as his people's high priest.

The presentation is rescued from artificiality by the writer's insistence on the experience and character of the historical Jesus. Jesus, who endured sore temptations on earth; Jesus, who learned by suffering how hard the path of obedience could be; Jesus, who interceded for his disciples that their faith might not fail in the hour of testing; Jesus, who offered up his life as a sacrifice on their behalf – this same Jesus remains the all-prevailing helper of those who come to God through him. It is because they have his example and abiding encouragement that the recipients of the letter are urged to sever their ties with an earth-bound cult and join the pilgrimage to that eternal and well-founded city "whose builder and maker is God" (Heb. 11:10).

If the writer of this letter was indeed Apollos, then Apollos was a very great man indeed. Certainly Apollos is a more likely candidate for the vacant authorship than most others who have been suggested. But this is not to say with assurance that the author was in fact Apollos. Apollos may indeed be the only Alexandrian Christian known to us from the New Testament age, but there could have been others, similarly gifted, whose names have not been preserved.

10. Concluding reflections

Apollos has left singularly little trace in Christian tradition. Jerome indeed mentions a tradition that he became bishop of Corinth, but no credence can be

given to this.[74] The inclusion of his name in later
lists of the seventy disciples of Luke 10:1ff. is a
patent anachronism. No apocryphal writing claims
him as author. When at last the Alexandrian church
wished to establish for itself a foundation which
brought it into association with the apostles, the
foundation which commended itself was not Apollos
of Alexandria, the friend of Paul, but Mark of
Jerusalem, the companion of Peter. For one short
spell Apollos flashes across the New Testament sky,
and then disappears into darkness as profound as
that from which he emerged.

But when we speak of darkness, we refer to our
own ignorance, not to the historical facts. Apollos
probably played a public part in early Christian life
for longer than we realize, but no further record of
it has survived.

Our source-material for the history of the apostolic
age is slender and selective. Thanks to the letters of
Paul and the historical work of Luke we can trace
certain phases of the progress of Christianity for a
period of three decades along the road leading from
Jerusalem *via* Antioch to Rome – but when we arrive
at Rome with Paul, the gospel has arrived there
before us. We can only guess how it got there. But
when we ask how it got to Alexandria, the situation
is still more obscure. Any attempt to reconstruct the
course of early Alexandrian Christianity, and of
Hellenistic Christianity in general, must reckon
seriously with the implications of the little we are

74. Jerome, *Commentary on Titus* 3:13 (Migne, *PL* 26.634B). Cf. the
early seventh-century *Chronicon Paschale*, ed. L. Dindorf (Bonn, 1832), i,
p. 402; ii, p. 126, where he appears not only as one of the seventy but
also as bishop of Caesarea.

told about Apollos, this cultured Alexandrian Jew with a mastery of the scriptures and an accurate knowledge of the story of Jesus, who for a brief space traverses the Pauline circle and endears himself to its members and their leader, makes a powerful impression on fellow-Jews and fellow-Christians in Ephesus and Corinth, and then vanishes from our sight.

CHAPTER 3

JAMES AND THE CHURCH OF JERUSALEM

1. The brethren of the Lord

The "brethren of the Lord" are recognized as an influential group in the primitive church.[1] Paul and Luke alike mention them alongside the apostles. According to Luke, they were closely associated with the apostles and other followers of Jesus in the days immediately following his resurrection (Acts 1:14); according to Paul, one of them, James, had actually seen the risen Christ (1 Cor. 15:7).

To any one who has read the gospels with some care, this is surprising: both the Markan and the Johannine traditions imply that the family of Jesus viewed his public activities with considerable reserve, while he himself declined to be restricted by the ties of blood-relationship: "Whoever does the will of God", he said, "is my brother, and. sister, and mother" (Mark 3:35). The fourth evangelist assures us that "even his brothers did not believe in him"

---

1. A classic treatment is J. B. Lightfoot, "The Brethren of the Lord", Dissertation II appended to *Saint Paul's Epistle to the Galatians* (London, 1865), pp. 251–291.

(John 7:5). How then did it come about that his relatives, who do not figure at all among his followers before his death, should so soon afterwards be found taking a leading place among them? It might have been expected that the disgrace of his execution would confirm in their minds the misgivings which they had felt about him all along. Paul's statement that in resurrection Jesus "appeared to James" provides an answer to our question. This experience evidently produced in James a revolutionary effect comparable to that which a similar experience later produced in Paul himself.

A later and legendary embellishment of the statement that the risen Christ "appeared to James" was given in *The Gospel according to the Hebrews*, as quoted by Jerome in the second entry of his work *On Illustrious Men*. According to this account James took an oath to eat no bread until he should see Jesus risen from the dead. When the risen Lord appeared to him, "he took bread and gave thanks and broke it, and then gave it to James the Just, saying to him, 'My brother, eat your bread, because the Son of Man has risen from those who sleep'."[2] (*The Gospel according to the Hebrews* was current among certain Jewish-Christian communities from the later second century onwards.)

It is not necessary to enter here into the precise relationship between "the brethren of the Lord" and the Lord himself. From the frequency with which they are mentioned along with his mother (Mark

2. Jerome, *De Viris Illustribus*, 2: this account, says Jerome, was derived from "the Gospel which is called 'According to the Hebrews' and was lately translated by me into the Greek and Latin speech – a work of which Origen also frequently makes use".

3:31 ff.//Matt. 12:46 ff.//Luke 8:19 ff.; Mark 6:3//Matt. 13:55; Acts 1:14) it might be inferred that they, like himself, were children of Mary;[3] the burden of proof rests on those who interpret the relationship differently.

Apart from Luke's general reference to "the brethren of the Lord" as included in the hundred and twenty who were in the apostles' company in Jerusalem in the days preceding the first Christian Pentecost (Acts 1:14 f.), his first specific mention of James comes in Acts 12:17, where Peter reports his escape from Herod Agrippa's prison to the believers who were praying together in Mary's house and tells them, before he leaves them, to pass the news on "to James and to the brethren". This implies that James and the brethren associated with him met in a different place from Peter's company – that they belonged, to use Pauline language, to a different house-church.[4]

But we have a reference to James at an earlier period in the history of the Jerusalem church in a document which antedates Acts by some decades – Paul's letter to the Galatians. There he tells his readers that, in the course of his visit to Jerusalem three years after his conversion "to get to know

---

3. Epiphanius (*Heresies*, 78) argued that they were children of Joseph by a previous wife. Then Helvidius of Rome restated the interpretation (already maintained by Tertullian and others) that they were children of Joseph and Mary, born after Jesus. In reply to Helvidius Jerome propounded a new theory: that they were the cousins of Jesus, children of Alphaeus by "Mary of Clopas", whom he inferred from John 19:25 to be the Virgin's sister (*Aduersus Heluidium de perpetua uirginitate beatae Mariae*). See the recent discussion in R. E. Brown, K. P. Donfried and others (ed.), *Mary in the New Testament* (London, 1978), pp. 65–72, 270–278, *et passim*.

4. See p. 28.

Kephas", he "saw none of the other apostles, except James the Lord's brother" (Gal. 1:18f.).[5] This may point to James as the second most important man in the church; at any rate, he was someone whom it was important for Paul to see. In the light of other indications, it may be inferred that even at this early date James was leader of one group in the Jerusalem church as Peter was leader of another.

In saying that he "saw none of the other apostles except James", Paul certainly indicates that he regarded James as an apostle. If we were compelled to understand his words otherwise, they could be construed differently – as though he meant, "I saw none of the other apostles, but I did see James the Lord's brother" – but this is a less natural construction to put on them.[6] Unlike Luke, Paul does not confine the designation "apostles" to the twelve. He claims to be an apostle himself, exercising an apostleship as valid as that of those who were apostles before him (cf. Gal. 1:17). Those who were apostles before him had evidently seen the risen Lord even if, like James, they were not included in the twelve. When, in his summary of resurrection

---

5. See p. 22.
6. Paul says ἕτερον δὲ τῶν ἀποστόλων οὐκ εἶδον, εἰ μὴ Ἰάκωβον τὸν ἀδελφὸν τοῦ κυρίου. J. B. Lightfoot's note says all that need be said: εἰ μή has (as always) exceptive force, the question here being "whether the exception refers to the whole clause or to the verb alone". In the present construction "the sense of ἕτερον naturally links it with εἰ μή, from which it cannot be separated without harshness, and ἕτερον carries τῶν ἀποστόλων with it" (*Saint Paul's Epistle to the Galatians*, pp. 84f.). Less probable is the translation offered by L. P. Trudinger (". . . A Note on Galatians i.19", *Novum Testamentum* 17 [1975], pp. 200–202): "other than the apostles I saw none except James the Lord's brother". According to Marius Victorinus, *In Epistulam Pauli and Galatas* . . . (on Gal. 1:19), the Symmachians (Ebionites) regarded this James as the twelfth apostle (ed. A. Locher [Leipzig, 1972], p. 14).

appearances, he says that Christ, having appeared
to Peter and then to the twelve, "appeared to James,
then to all the apostles" (1 Cor. 15:7), "all the
apostles" should certainly be interpreted as a wider
body than "the twelve" and equally certainly James
is to be regarded as one of those "apostles" as Peter
is one of "the twelve". The appearance of the risen
Lord to James was no doubt something of which
Paul heard from James himself during his first post-
conversion visit to Jerusalem just as he would have
heard of the appearance to Peter from Peter himself.

Paul, then, thought it valuable to establish personal
relations with James during that visit. Whether or
not he foresaw then the increasingly dominant rôle
which James would fill in Jerusalem there is no way
of knowing; but this increasingly dominant rôle is
documented by Paul and Luke independently.

2. *James's progress to leadership*

Next time Paul visited Jerusalem, James's leading
rôle had been established. When Paul tells how he
and Barnabas held a private conference with the
three leaders or "pillars" of the Jerusalem church,
he names them in the order: "James, Kephas and
John" (Gal. 2:9). Although Kephas (Peter) is the only
one of those three singled out for special mention in
the report of the conference, the order in which
their names are given tells its own story, which is
confirmed by the general impression made by all
the relevant evidence.[7]

7. See p. 29. It is, of course, possible that the sequence of names
corresponds to the order of precedence at the time of Paul's writing,
not at the time of the conference. So argues G. Klein, "Galater 2, 6–9

The private conference described by Paul in Gal. 2:1–10 was most probably later than Peter's imprisonment by Herod Agrippa. At the time of that imprisonment, if not earlier, James was evidently leader of one group in the Jerusalem church. Before many years had gone by, he was evidently acknowledged as a leader of that church as a whole. Paul's evidence to this effect is confirmed by Luke's account of the Council of Jerusalem – a later meeting, as has been suggested already, than the private conference of Gal. 2:1–10. The Council of Jerusalem was a meeting of the leadership of the Jerusalem church, with delegates from the church of Antioch in attendance, held to discuss not this time the delimitation of apostolic spheres of ministry but the terms on which Gentile converts might be admitted to church membership – in particular, whether they should be required to accept circumcision or not (Acts 15:5f.). According to Luke, after various people (including Peter) had spoken to the question, it was James who summed up the sense of the meeting and expressed his judgement in terms which those present agreed to adopt – the terms of the so-called Jerusalem decree.[8] It was James, rather than Peter, who could now carry the rank and file with him; this is an index of the confidence which James commanded in the Jerusalem church at large. James had not blotted his copy-book

---

und die Geschichte der Jerusalemer Urgemeinde", *ZTK* 57 (1960), pp. 275–295, especially pp. 282–286 (reprinted in G. Klein, *Rekonstruktion und Interpretation* [München, 1969], pp. 99–128, especially pp. 106–109); see reply by W. Schmithals, *Paul and James*, E. T. (London, 1965), p. 49, n. 31, p. 83, n. 13.

8. See p. 38.

by fraternizing with Gentiles, as Peter had done,[9] and he continued to enjoy the esteem not only of his more conservative brethren in the Jerusalem church but of pious Jerusalemites in general.

An opportunity for James's influence to increase at the expense of Peter's had already been provided when Peter left Jerusalem after his escape from Herod Agrippa's prison[10] – at least five years before the Council of Jerusalem. Perhaps, after that, Peter paid only occasional visits to Jerusalem and was no longer permanently resident there, as James was. But even when Peter was away from Jerusalem he was aware of James's influence and respected his wishes. This appears notably in his withdrawal from table-fellowship with Gentiles at Antioch when visitors "from James" conveyed their leader's message to him (Gal. 2:12).[11] These visitors need not be identified with the men who, according to Acts 15:1, went down from Jerusalem to Antioch and told the Gentile converts there that they could not be saved without circumcision. The latter visitors are said to have gone to Antioch on their own initiative. The letter sent to the churches of Syria and Cilicia in the name of "the apostles and elder brethren at Jerusalem"[12] (which embodied the Jerusalem decree) emphasized that those men had no mandate to teach as they did (Acts 15:23f.).

---

9. See p. 27.
10. See p. 28.
11. See p. 32.
12. Affinities in vocabulary and style have been traced between this letter and the Letter of James; cf. J. B. Mayor, *The Epistle of St. James* (London, ²1897), pp. iii f.; W. O. E. Oesterley, "The General Epistle of James", *The Expositor's Greek Testament*, ed. W. R. Nicoll, iv (London, 1910), pp. 391 f.

It is certain that the Jerusalem decree was promulgated by the mother church (and it is equally certain, in the light of Paul's writings, that Paul did not impose it on his own churches); and the Jerusalem church could not have promulgated it without James's approval. That it was actually promulgated on James's initiative, as Luke records, is entirely credible. Luke himself appears to have regarded it as a masterpiece of statesmanship.

3. Biblical exegesis at the Council of Jerusalem

It is specially interesting to mark the biblical support which James is said to have adduced for his initiative. Expressing approval of Peter's exhortation, based on personal experience, not to require from Gentile believers conditions which God himself had manifestly not required, James went on to say that the language of prophecy spoke to the same effect, as follows (Acts 15:15–18):

> "After this I will return,
> and rebuild David's fallen tent;
> I will rebuild its ruins
> and I will set it up,
> that the rest of mankind may seek the Lord,
> even all the Gentiles who are called by my name",
> says the Lord who makes this known from of old.

This is a quotation of Amos 9:11f., in a Greek version very close to that given by the Septuagint. In Acts the prefatory words "After this I will return"[13] replace the Septuagint "In that day"; in

13. Perhaps from Jer. 12:15.

Acts "the Lord" is the explicit object of "may seek",
whereas in the Septuagint the object of the verb is
left to be understood; Acts omits the phrase "as in
the days of old" found in the Septuagint after "I
will set it up," but adds "known from of old" at
the end of the quotation.[14]

In the context of the Council of Jerusalem, the
application of the oracle is clear: the Gentile mission
in its present form has been foretold by the prophets
of God with his manifest approval; no attempt
should therefore be made to turn Gentiles into Jews.
No disadvantage will be suffered by Moses: his law
is read publicly every sabbath in synagogues
throughout the world, and Gentiles who wish to
assume its yoke have every opportunity do so.[15] All
that is necessary to avoid giving offence to synagogue worshippers is for converts to Christianity to
accept certain social restrictions which will promote
smooth relations with Jews and especially with
Jewish Christians.

In its original setting the oracle quoted by James
holds out the promise that, although David's dynasty
has fallen on evil days, its past glories are nevertheless to be restored. In the heyday of David's imperial
power he had extended his sway over the Edomites
and other neighbouring ethnic groups. These became
not only David's vassals but also subjects of the God
of Israel, whom David worshipped and by whose

14. Without this addition the closing words of the Greek quotation
mean "says the Lord who does this"; with the addition, ποιῶν must be
translated "makes" – "says the Lord who makes this (known . . .)."
The addition may be borrowed from Isa. 45:21. Such minor additions
and similar variations possibly result from the conflation of *testimonia* in
a collection.
15. Acts 15:21.

help he won his victories.[16] The "shields of the earth" thus belonged to Yahweh: by his name the subject nations were called.[17] Hence the prophecy of restoration runs (in the Massoretic text):

> "In that day I will raise up
> the booth of David that is fallen,
> and repair its breaches,
> and raise up its ruins,
> and rebuild it as in the days of old;
> that they may possess the remnant of Edom
> and all the nations who are called by my name";
> says Yahweh who does this.

The Septuagint rendering of the prophecy presents a fine example of the spiritualizing tendency of that version. Instead of a programme of renewed imperial expansion the Septuagint rendering offers a picture of religious conversion. This is effected mainly by substitution of the vowels of *'ādām*, "mankind", for those of *'ĕdōm*, "Edom" (the consonants of the two Hebrew words are identical). In addition *yîr^ešû*, "may (re)possess", has been changed to *yidr^ešû*, "may seek"; this change may have originated as a scribal slip, but it helps the Septuagintal reinterpretation. The reinterpretation conveys a promise like that of Isa. 55:3f., where the fulfilment of the covenant mercies promised to David brings hope for the world at large, in keeping with Israel's mission to impart the knowledge of the true God to her neighbours. Whereas "the remnant of Edom" was the object of the verb "may possess" in the Hebrew

16. Ps. 18:43–48.
17. Ps. 47:8 f.

text, "the remnant of mankind" becomes the subject of the verb "may seek" in the Greek version,[18] where the unexpressed object of the verb is to be understood as "me" (i.e. the Lord, as the quotation in Acts explicitly says). The point of the Greek rendering, then, is that the nations will seek the God of Israel and voluntarily become his servants.

The application becomes still more precise in James's use of the oracle. The rebuilding of David's fallen tent has a more direct relevance than was possible for the pre-Christian translator. The "remnant of mankind" – that is, the non-Jewish nations – are yielding allegiance to the Son of David through hearing and obeying the gospel. The Son of David is extending his sovereignty over a wider empire than David himself ever controlled, and extending it by the persuasion of divine grace, not by force of arms. This and similar Old Testament oracles are now receiving a more comprehensive and detailed fulfilment than either the Hebrew prophets or even their Greek interpreters could have envisaged.

But is it historically probable that James, usually presumed to be a Hebrew and not a Hellenist, should have quoted the Septuagint version? Perhaps our accepted picture of James, and of other members of his family, is not so accurate as we imagine: it is based on very inadequate information. Even so, it is unlikely that James should have quoted the Septuagint when trying to persuade the more conservative members of the Jerusalem church. But the Septuagint rendering of Amos 9:11f. represents a spiritualizing

18. The accusative particle '*et*, which precedes *š*ᵉ*ērît* ("remnant") in Hebrew and indicates that that noun is the object, is ignored by the Greek translator.

interpretation which was current in the closing generations B.C., and there is no reason to exclude Judaea from the area of its currency. Even the Massoretic text foretells a day when "all the nations" that are called by the name of the God of Israel will submit to the sovereignty of the house of David[19] – and for all who were present at the Council of Jerusalem that sovereignty was embodied in Jesus, the Son of David.

Spiritualizing interpretations of the Hebrew text of this oracle were current around this time, as we know from the Qumran literature. In the Zadokite Work the raising up of David's fallen booth is interpreted of the re-establishment of the books of the Torah;[20] in the *Florilegium* from Qumran Cave 4 it is interpreted of the rising up of the offspring of David (i.e. the Messiah) in the latter days to save Israel.[21]

4. After the Council

After the Council of Jerusalem Luke has no more to say about Peter or any other member of the twelve. It appears that Peter and others of the twelve gave themselves to a more far-flung activity

19. Cf. H. A. W. Meyer, *Critical and Exegetical Handbook to the Acts of the Apostles*, E. T., ii (Edinburgh, 1881), p. 57; C. C. Torrey, *The Composition and Date of Acts* (Cambridge, Mass., 1916), pp. 38 f.

20. CD 7.15 f. This is a sectarian application: the re-establishment of the books of the Torah coincides with the rise of the covenant-community.

21. 4QFlor 1.11–13. In both the Qumran texts "I will raise up" is expressed by *waw* consecutive with the perfect (*wahᵃqîmôtî*) whereas the Massoretic text has the imperfect (*'āqîm*); it is doubtful if we should see here "a common textual tradition" with Acts 15:16 (καὶ ἀνοικοδομήσω, as against LXX ἀναστήσω), as is suggested by C. Rabin, *The Zadokite Documents* (Oxford, ²1958), p. 29.

from this time on. Indeed, Paul implies in 1 Cor.
9:5 that not only the apostles but the brethren of
the Lord also undertook itinerant ministry in the
eastern Mediterranean in the 50s. The one exception
was apparently James, who stayed in Jerusalem and
looked after the welfare of the church. The other
brethren of the Lord were married and, like the
apostles, were accompanied by their wives on their
missionary and pastoral journeys; James probably
remained unmarried – this would be all of a piece
with his general asceticism, which is fairly reliably
attested in later tradition.[22]

The church of Jerusalem, while it increased in
numbers during the thirty to forty years between its
formation and its dispersal on the eve of Titus's
siege of Jerusalem, seems at the same time to have
undergone a progressive narrowing in composition
and temper. The first narrowing was the result of
the scattering of the Hellenists after the death of
Stephen. About the same time, or shortly before,
Luke tells us that "a great many of the priests were
obedient to the faith" (Acts 6:7). Nothing more is
said about those priests. There has been considerable
speculation about them – had they, for example,
Essene sympathies?[23] We have no means of knowing.
Neither have we any means of knowing what the
influence of so many priestly converts was on the
outlook of the Jerusalem church as a whole.

On the eve of the Council of Jerusalem we are

22. Cf. Hegesippus, as quoted by Eusebius, *Hist.Eccl.* 2.23.4–7 (see
pp. 114 f).
23. As was suggested by C. Spicq, "L'épître aux Hébreux: Apollos,
Jean-Baptiste, les Hellénistes et Qumrân", *Revue de Qumran* 1 (1958–59),
pp. 365–390.

told of "some believers who belonged to the party of the Pharisees" (Acts 15:5). We are left in no doubt about their outlook: it was they who pressed unsuccessfully for the policy of circumcising Gentile converts.

Herod Agrippa's campaign against the apostles probably led to a further narrowing. If this campaign was encouraged by Peter's fraternizing with Gentiles, then plainly (in the eyes of many) such fraternizing was undesirable. Peter was too liberal for many of the Jerusalem Christians; indeed, James himself, by the standard of some of his followers, leant as far as was prudent in the liberal direction. There is much that must be read between the lines of Luke's account.[24] Luke, writing after the controversies of mid-century had died down, has no interest in recalling them beyond what is absolutely necessary, and emphasizes the very substantial area of agreement among the protagonists in those controversies rather than the points on which they differed.

About eight years after the Council of Jerusalem, when Paul paid his last visit to Jerusalem, he and his companions were received by James and the other elders who (according to Luke) painted a monochrome picture of the mother-church as it was by that time. "You see, brother", they said, "how many thousands[25] there are among the Jews of those who have believed; they are all zealous for the law" (Acts 21:20). The impression we get is that the

24. Cf J. J. Scott, Jr., "Parties in the Church of Jerusalem as seen in the Book of Acts", *Journal of the Evangelical Theological Society* 18 (1975), pp. 217–227.

25. Literally "tens of thousands" (μυριάδες), but this is hyperbole: the normal population of Jerusalem was probably not more than 60,000.

Jerusalem Christians were now, almost to the last
man, zealots for the law – the expression is not
unlike that which Paul uses to describe his own
character in his pre-Christian days when he says
that he was a "zealot" for his ancestral traditions
(Gal. 1:14).

This impression has been felt to conflict with that
made a few lines earlier in the narrative: "when we
had come to Jerusalem, the brethren received us
gladly" (Acts 21:17). Was it from the host of "zealots
for the law" that Paul and his companions received
such a warm welcome? Johannes Munck, "without
any authority in the manuscript[s]", as he admitted,
proposed to delete the words "of those who have
believed" from verse 20, reading in consequence:
"how many myriads there are in Judaea; they are all
zealots for the law" – the reference being to Jews in
general, not to Jewish Christians.[26] It is noteworthy
that Ferdinand Christian Baur, of the nineteenth-
century Tübingen school, with whose continuing
influence Munck takes issue throughout *Paul and the
Salvation of Mankind*, also (but for different reasons)
regarded the phrase "of those who have believed"
as spurious.[27] But such a conjectural emendation in
the face of all the textual evidence could be justified
only when the retention of the existing text is out
of the question; and that is by no means the
situation here.

We may take the text as it stands as evidence of
the progressive narrowing already recognized. It

26. J. Munck, *Paul and the Salvation of Mankind*, E. T. (London, 1959),
pp. 240f.
27. F. C. Baur, *Paul: his Life and Works*, E. T., i (London, ²1876), pp.
201–204.

could well be that this progressive narrowing was in part a protective reaction to the steady growth of militant sentiment and activity in Judaea – fostered by those who were, or were soon to be, known as Zealots in a distinctive sense.

5. *Greek gifts*

Reference has been made just now to Paul's last visit to Jerusalem. After the Council of Jerusalem, the only appearances made by the Jerusalem church in the writings of either Luke or Paul have to do with Paul's relations with that church.

Paul appears to have esteemed the Jerusalem church and its leaders more highly than they esteemed him. He visited the mother-church at important moments of transition in his apostolic carrer, and strove to maintain fellowship with it.[28] His apostolic commission, he insisted, was totally independent of Jerusalem, but it could not be properly discharged except in fellowship with Jerusalem. Any breach of that fellowship would go far to frustrate his ministry: it would mean, in his own words, that he had "run in vain" (Gal. 2:2).

According to Acts 18:22, Paul paid a brief visit to the church in Jerusalem between his Corinthian and Ephesian ministries (in the summer of A.D. 52).[29] But more importance attaches to his last visit to Jerusalem. Luke devotes considerable space to it and Paul

28. See W. L. Knox, *St. Paul and the Church of Jerusalem* (Cambridge, 1925).

29. "The church" of Acts 18:22 can be only the church of Jerusalem. The Western text of verse 21 is quite explicit: Paul says to the Ephesians, "I must by all means keep the coming festival in Jerusalem, and I will come to you again on my return, God willing".

makes it plain that it played a crucial part in his
missionary strategy. We can thus view this visit
through Luke's eyes (from his detailed record of it)
and through Paul's eyes (because he shares with his
readers the motives and hopes which led him to
undertake it, together with certain misgivings about
its outcome). But in our present context we should
like to be able to see it through the eyes of James
and his fellow-elders in the church of Jerusalem. To
see it – and to see it sympathetically – through their
eyes calls for an effort of historical imagination.

James and his colleagues knew that Paul's previous
visits to Jerusalem had regularly led to trouble, in
which others than himself were likely to be involved.
They knew that he had bitter enemies in the city,
and they knew that in their own Nazarene community there were those who utterly disapproved of
Paul's missionary policy – some of whom, indeed,
did what they could to invade his mission-field and
bring his Gentile converts over to what they regarded
as a better rule of faith and life.

Paul came to Jerusalem on this occasion bearing
gifts – gifts not from himself but from his churches
in the Greek-speaking world. The Jerusalem Christians are not likely to have known Virgil, but if
someone had quoted to them the words *timeo Danaos
et dona ferentes* ("I fear the Greeks even when they
bring gifts"), many of them would have said that
these words summed up their sentiments exactly.

What were those gifts? Luke makes one passing
reference to them when he represents Paul as saying
before the procurator Felix that after many years he
came to visit his nation "with alms and offerings"
(Acts 24:17). He says nothing more of them, perhaps

because he knew what unintended trouble sprang from them. Fuller and more precise information about them comes from Paul himself.

Over and above his desire to maintain good personal relations with the Jerusalem church, Paul was anxious that his Gentile churches should have a sense of solidarity with Jerusalem, and that this sense of solidarity should be reciprocated. To give practical effect to this, he organized in his Gentile churches on both sides of the Aegean Sea a collection for the relief of the poverty of their Jerusalem brethren. Paul had given an undertaking to do something of the kind at the end of the conference in which he and Barnabas had participated with the three Jerusalem leaders some ten years before: those leaders, he says, "asked us to remember 'the poor', and I made a special point of attending to this matter" (Gal. 2:10). "The poor" may have meant, quite literally, the poorer members of the Jerusalem church, but in due course the phrase came to denote its membership as a whole.[30] Paul had been engaged in this kind of Christian aid at an early stage in his apostleship, when he and Barnabas were deputed by the church of Antioch to take a monetary gift to the Jerusalem church in time of famine (Acts 11:30).[31]

At the later stage with which we are now concerned, Paul's hope was that involvement in a relief fund for Jerusalem would bring home to his Gentile converts their indebtness to the mother-

30. From this self-designation – Hebrew *hā'ebyônîm* ("the poor") – the Ebionites (see pp. 55 f., 116 ff.) derived their name.

31. It was, I believe, in the course of this famine-relief visit from Antioch that he and Barnabas had the meeting with the Jerusalem leaders described in Gal. 2:1–10.

church of Christendom, from which the gospel had
first begun to spread. He did not shrink from
encouraging a competitive spirit among his churches,
to see which of them would be foremost in
generosity and promptness. On the other hand, he
hoped that a generous gift from those churches
would persuade the Jerusalem church to think more
kindly of his Gentile mission. He knew that some of
the more conservative spirits in the Jerusalem church
had grave suspicions regarding himself and his
mission; others might be uneasy about giving him a
welcome because of the hostility felt towards him by
many non-Christian Jews in the city. Shortly before
he set out on his journey to Jerusalem he told the
Roman Christians in a letter that before he could
pay them a long-contemplated visit, he must first go
"to Jerusalem with aid for the saints", and besought
their prayers that this "service for Jerusalem may be
acceptable to the saints" (Rom. 15:25, 31). It was not
a foregone conclusion that all suspicions would be
allayed, but nothing (Paul might hope) would be
better calculated to allay them than a generous gift
from the Gentile churches, carried by living representatives of those churches.

Paul travelled by sea to Judaea with those representatives in the spring of A.D. 57, landed at Caesarea
and went up to Jerusalem. His friends at Caesarea
(who included Philip and his family) had arranged
that the party should be entertained in Jerusalem by
the Cypriot Mnason, who had been a member of
the mother-church from its inception.[32] When Luke

---

32. See p. 58. When Mnason is called "an early disciple" (ἀρχαῖος
μαθητής), it is implied that he had been a disciple from the beginning
(ἀπ᾽ ἀρχῆς).

(writing as one of the party) says that on their arrival in Jerusalem "the brethren received us gladly" (Acts 21:17), "the brethren" in question may have been Mnason and his associates.[33] If Mnason's house could accommodate Paul and his companions, it may have been the meeting-place of one of the groups in the Jerusalem church – a group comprising, perhaps, the few remaining Hellenists in the church, among whom the Gentile visitors might feel more at home than elsewhere in Jerusalem.

The day after their arrival in the city, says the narrator, "Paul went in with us to James; and all the elders were present. After greeting them, he related one by one the things that God had done among the Gentiles through his ministry. And when they heard it, they glorified God" (Acts 21:18–20).

They might well glorify God, for Paul told them how, through his preaching, many residents in the great cities of Macedonia, Achaia and proconsular Asia now acknowledged Jesus as Lord. By their submission to the sovereignty of Israel's Messiah, the rebuilding of David's fallen tent had been substantially advanced. And what Paul told them was corroborated by the presence of representative Gentile Christians, who presumably on this occasion presented to James and his colleagues the gifts which they had brought on behalf of their churches.

But were the gifts accepted? That may seem a strange question to ask, since gifts are usually accepted, especially by people in such economic

33. W. Schmithals, while he denies that these brethren were primarily Hellenists, says that the words "can only mean that the Jerusalem church as such received Paul gladly through its members present in Mnason's house" (*Paul and James*, p. 87).

straits as apparently beset the Jerusalem Christians.
But the question should be asked, partly because no
New Testament writer tells us that they were
accepted, and partly because some New Testament
students think it most likely that *"the Jerusalem church
refused to accept the collection"*.[34] Or, if they did not
refuse it outright, they postponed their acceptance
of it until Paul "had proved his good Jewish faith"
by falling in with the course of action proposed to
him by the elders.[35]

The reason for rejecting the gifts would be that
acceptance of them would be tantamount to expressing approval of Paul's Gentile mission. And if indeed
James and his colleagues planned to bring Christians
everywhere under the hegemony of the Jerusalem
church and its leadership,[36] Paul's planting of decen-
tralized churches in deliberate independence of Jerusalem must have been a major obstacle to that plan
and they could not even appear to approve of it.
But the evidence that James was party to such a
plan is scanty indeed.

The elders, however, were anxious about the
reaction of some of their flock – the numerous
"zealots for the law" – to the presence of Paul and
his friends. In the eyes of those "zealots", Paul's
refusal to impose the law and the customs on his
Gentile converts was bad enough, but they had

34. J. D. G. Dunn, *Unity and Diversity in the New Testament* (London,
1977), p. 257 (his italics); cf. A. J. Mattill, Jr., "The Purpose of Acts:
Schneckenburger reconsidered", in *Apostolic History and the Gospel*, ed.
W. W. Gasque and R. P. Martin (Exeter, 1970), p. 116.

35. J. D. G. Dunn, *ibid.*

36. As held, e.g., by E. Stauffer, *New Testament Theology*, E. T.
(London, 1955), p. 34. There probably was such a plan, but to ascribe
its promotion to James and his colleagues is to outrun the evidence.

heard rumours that he even dissuaded *Jewish* Christians from circumcising their sons and otherwise maintaining the holy traditions.[37] The elders dismissed those rumours as unfounded; they themselves had underwritten the Jerusalem decree which specifically exempted *Gentile* believers from the requirement of circumcision, while it stipulated certain "necessary things" which they should observe – and they felt that by making this concession they had gone as far as they could reasonably be expected to go.[38]

To forestall any trouble which might arise from their "zealous" brethren, the elders suggested that Paul should take part in a public ceremony which would demonstrate that he was a practising Jew. They invited him to join four of their number who had undertaken a Nazirite vow and were now due to discharge it, after undergoing some ritual purification.[39] If Paul would accompany those men into the temple precincts and pay their expenses, everyone would see that he was loyal to the law and that rumours to the contrary were false.

It is unlikely that Paul viewed this suggestion with the optimism expressed by its proponents; nevertheless, he went along with it. It was a matter of settled policy with him to live "as one under the law" in the company of those who were "under the law" (1 Cor. 9:29). As for a Nazirite vow, he had undertaken one himself at Corinth five years before

37. Paul's relaxed attitude to such matters, so far as Jewish Christians are concerned, may be inferred from 1 Cor. 7:17–19.

38. Cf. Acts 21:25.

39. The discharge of a Nazirite vow was a service of thanksgiving to God, e.g. for deliverance from some danger or other critical situation (cf. Num.6:1–21; Mishnah, tractate *Nazir*).

(Acts 18:18),[40] and to pay the expenses of others who had undertaken one was a recognized act of charitable piety.[41]

In any case, the outcome was disastrous. While Paul was carrying out his part in the ceremony, a hue and cry was raised against him by some Asian Jews who had come to Jerusalem for Pentecost and recognized him in the temple court; they charged him with violating the sanctity of the holy place by taking Gentiles into it.[42] He was attacked by a riotous mob and rescued in the nick of time by Roman soldiers from the adjoining Antonia fortress. The commanding officer took him into custody and, after some days, sent him to Felix at Caesarea. So inauspiciously ended Paul's last visit to the Jerusalem church.

A more sinister question than that about the acceptance of the Gentiles' gift has been raised about the proposal that Paul should accompany the four Nazirites to the temple. Did James and the elders foresee the danger that Paul would run and deliberately expose him to it? Did they, in fact, lure him into a trap? Was this their way of ensuring that, with Paul out of the way, there would be no serious obstacle to their plan to bring all the churches under their own control?

The question has not only been asked: it has been

40. It is most unlikely that it was Aquila who had undertaken this vow, as A. Ehrhardt held (*The Acts of the Apostles* [Manchester, 1969], p. 100).

41. The elder Herod Agrippa earned a reputation for piety by paying the expenses of many Nazirites (Josephus, *Ant.* 19.294).

42. Gentiles might not intrude beyond the outer court (therefore called the court of the Gentiles); this ban was underwritten by the Romans, who exceptionally allowed the Jewish authorities to pass and execute the death sentence for any breach of it.

answered with a decided Yes. Not only so; it has been held that Luke himself, being one of Paul's companions in Jerusalem, suspected "that Judaizers had drawn Paul into an ambush by luring him into the Temple".[43] But if "Judaizers" did this, those Judaizers were the elders themselves; and if Luke suspected this, his literary ministry of reconciliation must have been strained to breaking-point when, without a hint that their motives were ulterior, he portrays the elders as engaged in friendly conversation with Paul and suggesting the temple visit as a means of establishing his orthopraxy in the eyes of disaffected brethren.

Most of the Gentile Christians who came to Jerusalem with Paul no doubt made their way home as quickly and unobtrusively as possible. Even if their gifts were accepted, the turn of events which they had witnessed in Jerusalem must have gone far to frustrate Paul's hope that a bond of affection would be forged between them and their Judaean fellow-believers. And there is nothing to encourage us to suppose that the Judaean brethren felt more closely drawn to their Gentile fellow-Christians because their generous gifts manifested "the surpassing grace of God" (2 Cor. 9:14).

If the Jerusalem church and its leaders are exonerated (as, indeed, they must be) from the unworthy suspicions aroused by their ill-starred advice to Paul, it may be asked what exertions they made on his

43. A. J. Mattill, "The Purpose of Acts: Schneckenburger reconsidered" (see p. 106, n. 34), pp. 115 f.; cf. Y.–M. Park, *The Effect of Contemporary Conditions in the Jerusalem Church on the Writing of the Epistle to the Romans* (unpublished Ph.D. thesis, University of Edinburgh, 1979), pp. 204–213, 310–321.

behalf when they saw the trouble into which that advice had brought him. The answer must be that there was little they could do. They had no influence with the chief priests or the Sanhedrin.[44] Probably they felt relieved when Paul had been got away safely to Caesarea. It would be best, for the peace of the mother-church, if he never returned to Jerusalem. If the high priest and his colleagues were prosecuting him, it would be unwise to attract their unfriendly attention. It is easy to impute unworthy motives to James and his fellow-elders, but some attempt should be made to view the situation from within, as they had to do. For them it was a peculiarly delicate situation. They had to go on living in Jerusalem after Paul and other visitors had left. Moreover, if they were to persevere with their commission to evangelize their fellow-Jews, public association with Paul would have been a major handicap to their endeavours. It is possible, indeed, that even their limited association with him on this occasion had something to do with the illegal execution of James about five years later.

6. *The last days of James*

For the death of James in A.D. 62 our primary authority is Josephus, who was resident in Jerusalem at the time (being then in his middle twenties) and preserved an account of it in his *Antiquities*, written thirty to thirty-five years later. He tells how Festus,

44. J. D. G. Dunn suggests that "James's apparent high standing among orthodox Jews" might have been exploited in Paul's defence (*Unity and Diversity in the New Testament*, p. 256), but it is doubtful if this would have cut much ice with the Sanhedrin.

procurator of Judaea, died in office and was succeeded by Albinus. Since it took five weeks at least
for news to travel from Judaea to Rome, and five
weeks at least for the new procurator to travel from
Rome to Judaea, an interregnum of three months
elapsed between the death of Festus and the arrival
of his successor. Ananus (Annas) the younger, son
of an earlier high priest of the same name who
figures in the gospel story, had recently been
appointed high priest by Herod Agrippa II (in whose
gift the sacred office had been since A.D. 48). Ananus
was an impetuous and venturesome character, so
(says Josephus):

> thinking he had a suitable opportunity, with Festus
> now dead and Albinus still on the way, he convened
> a session of the judicial Sanhedrin and brought before
> this court James, the brother of Jesus the so-called
> Christ, and some other men. Accusing them of breaking
> the law, he handed them over to be stoned to death.
> Those men in the city who were reputed to be most
> fair-minded and strict in their regard for the law were
> angry at this. They sent a secret message to the king
> [Agrippa II], beseeching him to command Ananus to
> desist from such practices, for Ananus's action had
> been wrong from the beginning.[45]

Ananus, that is to say, violated the Roman prero-
gative by exercising capital jurisdiction on his own
initiative, and especially by having the death-sen-
tence executed on the spot, instead of waiting for
the procurator to arrive. Agrippa knew this, and put
himself in the right in the eyes of Rome by deposing

45. Josephus, *Ant.* 20.200 f.

Ananus there and then. Thus when Albinus arrived, angry at the news which had been dutifully reported to him, Agrippa could assure him that the offender had already been punished.

It is evident that the stoning of James was not so popular as the stoning of Stephen had been nearly thirty years before. James had not attacked the sanctity of the temple – had he done so, Ananus might have got away with his action – but James's assiduity in prayer within the holy precincts was a matter of public knowledge. It is impossible, however, to be sure about the nature of the crime with which James was charged.

One not very convincing suggestion is that James had played some part in the recent resistance of the ordinary priests (supported by leading citizens of Jerusalem) against the chief priests, who were blamed for oppressing them and depriving them of the tithes which were rightly theirs.[46] There is no evidence for this. James was a layman, not involved in priestly disputes, for all his regular attendance at the temple services. It is, besides, very doubtful if the Sanhedrin could have been persuaded to regard action in defence of victims of injustice as a capital crime: the chief-priestly group did not constitute a majority of the court.

Even so, the social injustice of those years, with the oppression of the poor by the wealthy landed aristocracy (including the chief-priestly families),

---

46. Cf. S. G. F. Brandon, "The Death of James the Just: A New Interpretation", in *Studies in Mysticism and Religion presented to G. G. Scholem* . . . , ed. E. E. Urbach, R. J. Zwi Werblowsky, C. Wirazubski (Jerusalem, 1967), pp. 57ff. The conflict over the tithes is mentioned by Josephus, *Ant.* 20.181, 205–207.

could provide an appropriate life-setting for the New Testament document called the Letter of James. There is much in its content that reads very well as if it could be the work of James the Just, with its emphasis on self-control, righteousness, mercy, impartiality, poverty and patience, and its excoriation of hypocrisy, partiality and exploitation of the weak. One feature that has given pause to readers who might otherwise be ready to ascribe it to our James is its Greek style. While its message is delivered with the moral fervour of Old Testament prophecy at its most searing, with a dash of the Sermon on the Mount thrown in, its style is that of the classical Cynic-Stoic diatribe.

An attractive suggestion was once made by F. C. Burkitt, to the effect that the later Greek church of Aelia Capitolina, the Emperor Hadrian's new foundation on the site of old Jerusalem, "rather like a new purchaser that has bought the Old Manor House, who after a while begins to collect old family portraits and souvenirs", rescued from oblivion the text of an Aramaic discourse delivered by James the Just and produced the free Greek rendering which has come down to us as the Letter of James.[47]

The death of James must have been a demoralizing blow to the church which he had guided so conscientiously and wisely for fifteen difficult years. In fact the church of Jerusalem never recovered from the blow. Another member of the family of Jesus was in due course elected to fill James's place. But

---

47. F. C. Burkitt, *Christian Beginnings* (London, 1924), pp. 65–71. This reconstruction sets a question-mark against arguments from the resemblances in wording between the apostolic letter of Acts 15:23–29 and the Letter of James (see p. 92, n. 12).

in a few years the church of Jerusalem left its home
city, about the time of the outbreak of the Jewish
revolt against Rome, and migrated to the district of
Pella and to other places in Transjordan and Egypt.
Henceforth the original church of Jerusalem was the
church in dispersion.[48] There is perhaps one reference
in the New Testament to the dispersion of the
mother-church – the pictorial reference in Rev. 12:6,
where she is portrayed as the woman who "fled
into the wilderness, where she has a place prepared
by God".

7. *Later developments*

Another and more detailed account of James's trial
and execution is provided by the Palestinian Christian writer Hegesippus (*c.* A.D.170), excerpts from
whose writings, including this account, are preserved
by Eusebius in his *Ecclesiastical History*. Unfortunately
this account is so full of legendary embellishments,
and draws so lavishly on Luke's record of the death
of Stephen, that it is difficult to decide where
genuine tradition ends and fantasy begins.

According to Hegesippus, James's ascetic life and
strict devotion to prayer and temple-worship earned
him the reverence of the Jerusalem populace, who
called him James the Just and "bulwark of the
people". He won many Jews to the Nazarene Way
by his manner of life and his earnest testimony to
Jesus. A deputation from the Sanhedrin waited on
him and posed the enigmatic question: "What is the
door of Jesus?" – meaning perhaps "the door of
which Jesus spoke" (cf. John 10:9) or "the door of

48. Cf. the address to "the twelve tribes in the Dispersion" in Jas.
1:1.

salvation".[49] Angered by his response, they set him
on a pinnacle of the temple and repeated their
question. He replied, "Why do you ask me again
about the Son of Man? He sits at the right hand of
the Almighty in heaven and he will come on the
clouds of heaven." This led many of the surrounding
multitude to glorify God and cry, "Hosanna to the
Son of David!" The rulers then realized their mistake
in giving James such an opportunity for public
witness, and they began to shout in protest, "Oho!
even the just one has fallen into error." They then
seized him, threw him down and began to stone
him. Like Stephen, he prayed for his executioners,
and one of the priests, a Rechabite, called out,
"Stop! What are you doing? The just one is praying
for you." But a fuller lifted up the club which he
used in his daily work and brought it down on
James's head, killing him. And immediately, says
Hegesippus, Vespasian besieged them.[50]

This last remark probably reflects a popular belief
that, when James's constant intercession was so
violently brought to an end, the city was doomed;
the eight-years interval between the death of James
and the siege of Jerusalem has been telescoped.[51]

49. There is a close resemblance between Hebrew *yᵉšû'āh* ("salvation")
and *yēšûa'* ("Jesus").

50. Quoted by Eusebius, *Hist. Eccl.* 2.23.4–18. Clement of Alexandria,
Hypotyposes 6 (quoted by Eusebius, *Hist. Eccl.* 2.1.5), speaks of "James
the Just, who was thrown down from the pinnacle of the temple and
beaten to death with a fuller's club", but he is probably dependent on
Hegesippus.

51. We may compare the popular interpretation of Antipas's military
defeat by Aretas in A.D. 36 as a judgement for his execution of John
the Baptist seven or eight years before (Josephus, *Ant.* 18.114–119), or
the interpretation of Pompey's assassination in 48 B.C. as a judgement
for his sacrilegious intrusion into the holy of holies in Jerusalem fifteen
years before (Ps.Sol. 2.30–32).

For the rest, when the embellishments are stripped off, the story amounts to this: the high priest and his colleagues, alarmed at the growth of militant messianism, which threatened to embroil the nation with the Roman power, demanded that James should disown his Nazarene claim that Jesus was the Messiah. His refusal to do so led to his death.

Another legendary embellishment in Hegesippus's account represents James as wearing priestly vestments and having the right to enter the sanctuary (the holy house itself, as distinct from the temple courts).[52] In the literal sense, of course, this is impossible; James did not belong to the tribe of Levi and so could not have been granted any priestly privileges. It is probably an allegorical expression of his steadfast intercessory ministry; it perhaps also reflects the belief held by some Jewish Christians, that James and his successors in the leadership of the Jerusalem church, by virtue of their relationship to Jesus, were the true high priests of the new Israel, ministrants in the spiritual temple composed of living stones.[53]

The source of Hegesippus's account appears to have been an Ebionite *Acts of the Apostles* (a counterpart to Luke's work), which narrated "the things done by the twelve apostles in the presence of the people in the temple".[54] This work is referred

---

52. Hegesippus, as quoted by Eusebius, *Hist. Eccl.* 2.23.6.
53. Cf. A. Ehrhardt, *The Apostolic Succession* (London, 1953), pp. 64 f.
54. This quotation sums up the contents of the seventh book of the *Preachings of Peter*, an Ebionite work in ten books (*Clementine Recognitions* 3.75). The Ebionite *Acts* probably served as a source for the *Preachings of Peter*, as these *Preachings* in turn served as a source for the pseudo-Clementine literature.

to in patristic literature,[55] but it has not been preserved in its original form: it has been largely incorporated in what is called the pseudo-Clementine literature.[56] One section of these Ebionite *Acts* dealt with "the ascents of James"[57] – the occasions, presumably, when he went up to the temple and disputed with the chief-priestly establishment, maintaining (in accordance with later Ebionite teaching) that it should be treated as a house of prayer and not as a place of animal sacrifice.

In later Ebionite tradition James figures as bishop of the holy church, the custodian and guarantor of the authentic tradition of Jesus. While he is not one of the twelve he is, if anything, superior to them: it is to him, for example, that Peter has to render an account of his apostolic service. He is assisted by a college of elders, who bear much the same relation to him as the members of the Sanhedrin before A.D. 70 bore to the high priest, their *ex officio* president.

Some features of this tradition can be recognized as an exaggerated development of tendencies already discernible in the New Testament. In so far as the Ebionites had any time for Paul – and for the most part they seem to have stigmatized him as the "enemy" who sowed tares among the wheat[58] – they probably maintained that he, as well as Peter, was accountable to James and his colleagues: does not Luke himself relate how Paul and Barnabas reported

55. E. g. Epiphanius, *Heresies* 30.16.7.

56. That is, the *Clementine Recognitions* and *Clementine Homilies*, fictitiously ascribed to Clement of Rome. See pp. 25, 116.

57. Epiphanius, *Heresies* 30.16.7.

58. In the pseudo-Clementines Simon Magus, the untiring opponent of Peter, is at times a thin disguise for Paul.

to the Jerusalem apostles and elders "all that God had done with them" (Acts 15:4) and how Paul, at a later date, gave James and the elders a detailed account of "the things that God had done among the Gentiles through his ministry" (Acts 21:19)?

Not all the Jewish Christians in dispersion were Ebionites, but it was the Ebionites who looked back to James as their apostle extraordinary. Unlike the followers of Peter, they did not foster amicable relations with the followers of Paul. They were increasingly written off as heretics by mainstream Christianity, partly (there is some reason for believing) because they took into their system elements of Essenism and other strands of Jewish nonconformity.[59] But for generations they continued to regard themselves as the true mother-church of Christendom, guardians of the truth as it is in Jesus, accepting the leadership of his family – the brethren of the Lord and their descendants – so long as any survived. They might be written off as heretical and schismatic, but this did not shake their assurance that they were the true Israel and that the Gentile churches were as apostate in one direction as normative Judaism was in the other.[60] Against both they maintained their polemic, until whatever remnants were left of them by the seventh century were swamped in the rising flood of Islam. But to the end they venerated the memory of James the Just,

---

59. Cf. O. Cullmann, "Die neuentdeckten Qumran-Texte und das Judenchristentum der Pseudoklementinen", in *Neutestamentliche Studien für Rudolf Bultmann*, ed. W. Eltester (BZNW 21, 1954), pp. 35–51.

60. The major treatment of this subject is H. J. Schoeps, *Theologie und Geschichte des Judenchristentums* (Tübingen, 1949). An appendix to this work (pp. 381–456) deals in detail with the Ebionite *Acts of the Apostles*.

"for whose sake", according to one estimate of his significance, "heaven and earth were made".[61]

---

61. *Gospel of Thomas*, saying 12: "The disciples said to Jesus, 'We know that you are going to leave us: who will be chief over us?' Jesus said to them, 'In the place to which you go, betake yourselves to James the Just, on whose behalf heaven and earth alike were made'." This Egyptian compilation is manifestly dependent (at this point at least) on a Jewish-Christian (probably Ebionite) source.

CHAPTER 4

JOHN AND HIS CIRCLE

1. The memory of John at Ephesus

The first effective evangelization of the province of Asia was undertaken during the two-and-a-half to three years when Paul made his headquarters at Ephesus, from the summer of A.D. 52 to the spring of A.D. 55. So effectively was this work carried out at that time, by Paul and his colleagues, that "all the residents of Asia heard the word of the Lord, both Jews and Greeks" (Acts 19:10). Before Paul started his ministry there, there were "disciples" in Ephesus, and perhaps in other cities of proconsular Asia, defective as their knowledge of the Way may have been;[1] but their Christian influence was minimal by comparison with his. Also, as we have seen, the address of 1 Peter probably bespeaks some contact of Peter with Asia Minor,[2] but Peter's name plays no part in the Christian tradition of that area.

Indeed, even the name of Paul plays but a minor part in the Christian tradition of Ephesus and other

1. See p. 70.
2. See p. 32.

cities of Asia. The dominant name from the apostolic age which dominates Asian, and especially Ephesian, tradition is that of John. The dominance of John's name calls for explanation, but so does the eclipse – partial eclipse at least – of Paul's name.

For the eclipse of Paul's name we are prepared here and there in the later parts of the New Testament. It is reflected both in Paul's speech to the Ephesian elders in Acts 20:29 f., where he predicts attacks from without and subversion from within their church, and in 2 Tim. 1:15: "you are to know that all Asia has fallen away from me." A landslide away from Paul's teaching and authority is implied. We are imperfectly informed about its nature. The letter to the Colossians bears witness to one untoward development in the province at an earlier date, and others are hinted at elsewhere in the Pastoral Epistles.[3]

The later sixties of the first century, however, saw a welcome revitalizing of the gospel testimony in some parts of the province. This was due to the immigration of a number of Christians from Judaea shortly before the Jewish revolt of A.D. 66. These were for the principal part not the more conservative members of the Jerusalem church (many of whom, about the same time, migrated east of the Jordan), but outward-looking members of the church of Caesarea and other churches in the succession to those Hellenistic believers who, forced to quit Jerusalem in the persecution that broke out after Stephen's death, launched the Gentile mission in the adjoining regions.[4]

3. E.g. 1 Tim. 1:6 f., 19 f.; 4:1–3; 2 Tim 2:17 f.; 4:3 f.; Tit. 1:10–16.
4. See pp. 57 ff.

Those who migrated to proconsular Asia included
some very eminent Christians – Philip the evangelist
and his daughters, for example, whose tombs were
pointed out some generations later at Hierapolis in
Asian Phrygia,[5] and "John the disciple of the Lord",
whom tradition associates mainly with Ephesus. The
esteem accorded to his memory in the tradition
suggests his identification with John the son of
Zebedee, one of the twelve: in the vocabulary of the
Fourth Gospel the twelve are not called apostles,
but simply disciples. Although he was in no sense
a founder of the Ephesian church he soon came to
enjoy in that church the kind of prestige that Peter
and Paul enjoyed in Roman tradition.

One visible token of this Ephesian tradition may
be seen today on the hill of Ayasoluk, where stand
the very substantial and impressive remains of the
basilica erected by the Emperor Justinian (A.D.
527–565) in honour of St. John the divine. This
designation survives, in a corrupt form, in the name
of the place, for Ayasoluk goes back to Greek *hágios
theológos*, the "holy divine". Ayasoluk was indeed
the name of the town standing at the foot of the
hill until the expulsion of Greeks from Anatolia in
1923, when it was replaced by the Turkish name
Selçuk (which has the advantage of rhyming with
Ayasoluk and sharing four of its phonemes).

In Christian Ephesus the basilica of St. John
enjoyed for centuries something like the renown
which the temple of Artemis had enjoyed in pagan
Ephesus. Procopius, who tells of Justinian's building

5. Polycrates and Proclus in Eusebius, *Hist. Eccl.* 3.31.3, 4; cf. 3.39.9.
According to Polycrates as quoted in *Hist. Eccl.* 5.24.2, one of the
daughters was buried in Ephesus.

it, says that "it resembles, and is in all respects a rival to, the church which he dedicated to all the apostles in the imperial city"[6] (Constantinople) and describes it as "the most sacred shrine in Ephesus and one held in special honour".[7]

The basilica was severely damaged in the invasion of the Seljuk Turks in 1090. The site on which its ruins stood was excavated in 1927 and the following years by Austrian archaeologists, who discovered that Justinian's building was erected around an earlier square church, the cross-vault of which rested on four slender columns.[8] This earlier church was built probably in the fourth century – by Theodosius I or even by Constantine the Great. If the analogy of the well-known Constantinian foundations in Rome and Jerusalem is relevant, the site on the hill of Ayasoluk would have been chosen because of a belief or tradition that St. John was buried there. And in truth beneath the fourth-century church there was found a system of subterranean vaults, one of which lay directly under the altar. At one time these vaults could be entered by a steep and narrow stepped passage, which was later blocked up, except for an air-shaft the exit of which was close by the altar. Whether or not it had been blocked up before the Council of Ephesus in 431, it was for more serious reasons than this that the Syrian bishops

6. Procopius, *Buildings* 5.1.6.

7. Procopius, *Secret History* 3.1.

8. J. Keil, "XIII Vorläufiger Bericht über die Ausgrabungen in Ephesus", *Jahreshefte des österreichischen archäologischen Instituts in Wien* 24 (1929), Beiblatt, cols. 8–67 (especially 52–67); "XIV Vorläufiger Bericht . . .", *Jahreshefte* . . . 25 (1929), Beiblatt, cols. 5–52 (especially 5–21). See also "Die Wiederauffindung des Johannesgrabes in Ephesus", *Biblica* 13 (1932), pp. 121 ff. Procopius (*Buildings* 5.1.5) mentions the earlier shrine, but says it was built by "the natives" (οἱ ἐπιχώριοι).

who were present there complained that, after travelling such distances, they were unable to worship at the tomb of "the thrice-blessed John, divine and evangelist, who was granted such close access to our Saviour".[9]

Some years before the Council of Ephesus, Augustine of Hippo reported a rumour that the earth above John's tomb at Ephesus visibly moved up and down, as though someone were breathing there below.[10] If the Syrians who attended the Council knew of this rumour, they may have been all the more disappointed at not being able to verify it for themselves.

It is long since there was a Christian community in that area to worship at the tomb of John, but the basilica enjoyed a moment of latter-day glory in 1967 when Pope Paul VI paid it a visit and, as an

9. E. Schwartz (ed)., *Acta Conciliorum Oecumenicorum*, i. 5 (Berlin/Leipzig, 1927), p. 128. R. Eisler (*The Enigma of the Fourth Gospel* [London, 1938], p. 124) suggests that it was the blocking up of the tomb that was the obstacle, but their letter implies that they were deliberately prevented from worshipping not only there but at other Ephesian martyr-tombs. The council was held in the great church of St. Mary (actually twin churches) – appropriately, when one considers that this council gave official confirmation to the Virgin's designation *Theotokos*. By the time of the council popular Christian belief in Ephesus, identifying the John who had resided there with the beloved disciple who took the Virgin "to his own home" after Jesus from the cross entrusted her to his care (John 19:26 f.), held that she accompanied the disciple to Ephesus and spent her closing years there. In a public announcement of the condemnation of Nestorius the council described itself as meeting "in the [city] of the Ephesians, where John the divine and the holy Virgin Mary, the *Theotokos*, [had been]" (Schwartz *ACO*, i.2 [Berlin/Leipzig. 1927], p. 70). Since 1891 a building in Panaya Kapulü, about a mile distant from the city, has been venerated as the house of Mary as seen in vision and described in detail by the stigmatic Westphalian nun Katherina von Emmerick (1774–1824). This place of modern pilgrimage, staffed by Capuchins, has never received official ecclesiastical recognition, although it was visited by Pope Paul VI in 1967.

10. Augustine, *Homilies on the Gospel of John*, 124.

inscription in Turkish and Latin records, prayed (*preces effudit*) at the sacred spot.

2. John the divine

Who is John the divine – the *theologos* – who gave his designation to the hill and the neighbouring village?

To readers of the English Bible the designation "John the divine" is associated with the last book of the New Testament, entitled in the Authorized and Revised Versions "The Revelation of St. John the Divine" – following the precedent of a number of mediaeval manuscripts.[11] But when the designation "the divine" was attached to St. John in particular, not earlier (so far as one can tell) than the third century, it was attached to the Evangelist, the author of the Logos-prologue, rather than to the seer of Patmos. If the Evangelist was identical with the seer of Patmos, good and well: we should simply say then that the designation was given to him rather as the Evangelist than as the seer of Patmos.[12] This question of identity is not our primary concern here, but we must observe that, of the five "Johannine" documents in the New Testament, the Revelation is the only one which expressly claims to have been written by a man named John (the other four are anonymous). In the early Christian centuries, however, John the seer of Patmos was generally identi-

11. See B. M. Metzger, *A Textual Commentary on the Greek New Testament* (London/New York, 1971), p. 731.

12. The oldest attested occurrences of ὁ θεολόγος applied specifically or *par excellence* to the Fourth Evangelist appear in fragments of Origen's commentary on the Gospel of John (*GCS*, iv, pp. 483, 484, 485).

fied with John the apostle, the son of Zebedee, with the Fourth Evangelist and with "the disciple whom Jesus loved" mentioned repeatedly in the closing chapters of the Fourth Gospel.[13] Those who were unable to identify the seer of Patmos with the Fourth Evangelist, whether on literary grounds (like Dionysius of Alexandria) or on theological grounds (like Eusebius of Caesarea), were exceptions.[14]

3. The witness of Polycrates

In the debate about the proper observance of Easter towards the end of the second century in which the protagonists were Polycrates, bishop of Ephesus, and Victor, bishop of Rome (c. 189–199), Polycrates defends the antiquity of the quartodeciman practice – the practice of observing Easter on the fourteenth day of the appropriate lunar month,[15] after the Jewish tradition, regardless of the day of the week on which it fell. He invokes the authority of the great *stoicheia* (i.e. in effect, Christians of the apostolic age)[16] who died and were buried in the province of Asia. Among these he mentions "John, who leaned on the Lord's breast, who was a priest wearing the mitre, and a witness and teacher: he sleeps at Ephesus".[17] Here the John who settled in Asia is

13. John 13:23; 19:25–27; 20:2–10; 21:20–24. At the end of the last of these passages he is described further as "the disciple who is bearing witness to these things, and who has written these things".

14. See pp. 135 f., 138 f.

15. The Jewish month of Nisan, the Macedonian month of Artemisios (corresponding to March/April in the Julian calendar).

16. The word στοιχεῖα (which primarily means "letters of the alphabet" and then "elements") may here be understood as "luminaries" (from its use in the sense of sun, moon, etc.), i.e. "people of distinction".

17. Quoted by Eusebius, *Hist. Eccl.* 3.31.3; 5.24.2.

identified with the beloved disciple who, in the fourth evangelist's account of the Last Supper, reclined next to Jesus on that occasion and asked who his betrayer was (John 13:23–25). The statement that he was "a priest wearing the mitre" gives one pause. The *petalon* (for that is the Greek word here), as used in the Septuagint, is not the high-priestly mitre itself but the plate of gold attached to it, which bore the inscription "Holy to Yahweh".[18] This was worn by the high priest only, not by any of the ordinary priests. What Polycrates understood by it is uncertain. It might be a simple error, arising possibly from a confusion of John the disciple with that John who, according to Acts 4:6, was "of the high-priestly family". (This high-priestly John is otherwise unknown, unless we follow the Western text and read "Jonathan"; if so, he is presumably to be identified with Jonathan son of Annas, who occupied the high-priesthood for a few months in A.D. 36–37 in succession to Caiaphas.)[19]

On the other hand, the language might be (and more probably is) figurative, in which case we are reminded of Hegesippus's statement that James the Just "alone was permitted to enter the sanctuary, for indeed he did not wear wool but linen".[20] This seems to ascribe to James priestly, if not high-

18. Exodus 28: 36 (LXX 31).

19. Josephus, *Ant.* 18.95,123; 19.313 ff.; 20. 162 ff. R. Eisler identified the high-priestly John of Acts 4:6 with Theophilus, son of Annas, who succeeded his brother Jonathan as high priest in A.D. 37 and was removed by Herod Agrippa I four years later (Josephus, *Ant.* 18.123; 19.297); he identified this John further with Polycrates's wearer of the πέταλον and with the disciple of John 18:15 f. who was "known to the high priest" (*The Enigma of the Fourth Gospel*, pp. 39–45. 52 f.). See pp. 148 f. below.

20. Quoted by Eusebius, *Hist. Eccl.* 2.23.6; see p. 116.

priestly, privileges which certainly did not belong to him by birth and which therefore are more probably to be interpreted metaphorically. The *petalon* which, according to Polycrates, John wore might have a similar metaphorical significance.

4. *The witness of Irenaeus*

Other writers more or less contemporary with Polycrates assume rather than assert John's Ephesian connection. Clement of Alexandria, for example, says that after Domitian's death (A.D. 96) "John the apostle" moved from the island of Patmos to Ephesus – a statement which may go back to Hegesippus.[21] About the same time Irenaeus, in his treatise *Against Heresies*, calls the church of Ephesus "a true witness to the tradition of the apostles" since not only was it founded by Paul but it also provided a home for John, who remained there until the time of Trajan.[22]

By the time Irenaeus wrote this treatise he was bishop of Lyons in Gaul, but he was a native of the province of Asia and spent the first part of his life there. In his younger days he had known Polycarp, bishop of Smyrna, who died a martyr-death at an advanced age in 156.[23] Polycarp, he says, "was not only taught by apostles and enjoyed the company of many who had seen Christ, but was also appointed

21. Clement, *Quis diues saluetur* 42 (quoted by Eusebius, *Hist. Eccl.* 3. 23.6). The case for seeing the authority of Hegesippus behind this statement is presented by H. J. Lawlor, *Eusebiana* (Oxford, 1912), pp. 51 ff.

22. Irenaeus, *Against Heresies* 3.3.4.

23. The date (23 February 156) preferred by C. H. Turner, "The Day and Year of St. Polycarp's Martyrdom", *Studia Biblica et Ecclesiastica*, ii (Oxford, 1890), pp. 105 ff.

by apostles in Asia bishop of the church in Smyrna".[24] The generalizing plural "apostles" is used here in an extended sense (meaning perhaps those who had seen the Lord), but Irenaeus makes it plain that the apostle whom he has particularly in mind is John.

Irenaeus's most circumstantial reference to Polycarp's acquaintance with John comes in his letter to Florinus, a friend of earlier days who (in Irenaeus's eyes) had deviated from the true faith. He reminds Florinus how in their youth they had both frequented Polycarp's house.

> I remember the events of those days more clearly than those of more recent date, . . . so that I can speak of the very place where the blessed Polycarp sat and held discourse. I can tell how he went forth and came in, the manner of his life and his bodily appearance, the discourses which he addressed to the people. I can recall how he reported his companionship with John and with the others who had seen the Lord, how he recorded their words and what things he heard from them about the Lord, concerning his miracles and teaching. Polycarp received these things from those who were eyewitnesses of the word of life[25] and reported them all in conformity with the scriptures.[26]

Irenaeus's birth, on various grounds, cannot well be dated after A.D. 140; he would have been in his teens when he sat at Polycarp's feet and, as he himself says, impressions formed at that age remain tenaciously and vividly in the memory even (or

24. Irenaeus, *Against Heresies* 3.3.4.
25. Cf. Luke 1:2; 1 John 1:1.
26. Quoted by Eusebius, *Hist. Eccl.* 5.20.4 ff.

indeed especially) when more recent recollections
begin to fade.

Irenaeus, like Polycrates, wrote to Pope Victor
about the Easter controversy and affirmed that
Polycarp had always followed the quartodeciman
reckoning "in company with John the disciple of the
Lord and the other apostles with whom he
associated".[27]

It has been held against Irenaeus's account of
Polycarp that Pionius's *Life of Polycarp*, composed
around A.D. 250, has nothing to say of Polycarp's
association with John.[28] But even if the Pionian *Life*
is not so completely fictitious as J. B. Lightfoot
supposed it to be,[29] it cannot be compared for
evidential value with the testimony of Irenaeus, and
Pionius's strong anti-quartodeciman convictions
would be sufficient to make him keep silent about
John, who was invoked as the highest authority for
quartodeciman practice.[30]

5. *The witness of Papias*

Another witness from the last decades of the
second century is the anti-Marcionite prologue to the
Fourth Gospel.[31] The original Greek of this prologue

27. Quoted by Eusebius, *Hist. Eccl.* 5.24.16.

28. Cf. B. H. Streeter, *The Primitive Church* (London, 1929), pp. 94 f.,
111 f., 265 ff.

29. J. B. Lightfoot, *Ignatius and Polycarp*, iii (London, 1883), pp. 433
ff., 488 ff.

30. Cf. C. J. Cadoux, *Ancient Smyrna* (Oxford, 1938), pp. 305 ff., 374
ff.

31. The anti-Marcionite origin and character of this and companion
prologues was first established by D. de Bruyne, "Les plus anciens
prologues latins des Evangiles", *Revue Bénédictine* 40 (1928), pp. 193 ff.;
it has been called in question by J. Regul, *Die antimarcionitischen
Evangelienprologe* (Freiburg, 1969).

has disappeared: its text survives in a corrupt form in a Latin version which may be rendered thus:

> The Gospel of John was published and given to the churches by John while he was still in the body, as a man of Hierapolis, Papias by name, John's dear disciple, has related in his five *exegetical* books.[32] He indeed copied the Gospel accurately at John's dictation. But the heretic Marcion was thrust out by John, after being repudiated by him for his contrary views. He had carried writings or letters to him from brethren who were in Pontus.

The reference to Marcion is corrupt: it was probably to Papias, but certainly not to John, that he came from Pontus, and Papias evidently disowned him as forthrightly as Polycarp did.[33] As for the statement that Papias was "John's dear disciple" and served him as amanuensis, this is chronologically possible and nothing that we know for certain rules it out of court. However, the author of the prologue was dependent on Papias for his information and it is possible, as Lightfoot suggested, that he misread Papias's "they copied" (meaning members of John's school) as "I copied".[34]

32. Lat. *in exotericis (id est in extremis) quinque libris.* It is assumed here that the Greek text ran ἐν τοῖς πέντε ἐξηγητικοῖς βιβλίοις, that ἐξηγητικοῖς was corrupted to ἐξωτερικοῖς, which was duly translated into Latin as *externis*, and that in the Latin transmission *externis* was further corrupted to *extremis* (cf. J. B. Lightfoot, *Essays on the Work Entitled "Supernatural Religion"* [London, 1889], p. 213).

33. Polycarp, who had known him earlier in Asia Minor, recognized him in Rome in A.D. 154 as "the first-born of Satan" (Irenaeus, *Against Heresies* 3.3.4).

34. J. B. Lightfoot, *Essays on the Work Entitled "Supernatural Religion"*, p. 214. The forms of the first person singular and the third person plural would be identical in the imperfect (ἀπέγραφον) and very similar in the aorist (ἀπέγραψα, ἀπέγραψαν), especially if the final ν was

As for Papias's own words about John, they survive in one famous fragment quoted by Eusebius – a fragment to be dated half a century earlier than any of the testimonies quoted thus far.

Papias, bishop of Hierapolis in the Lycus valley in the first half of the second century, was contemporary with Polycarp. According to Irenaeus, he was a companion of Polycarp and, like him, "a hearer of John";[35] but Eusebius, after quoting Irenaeus to this effect, says that Papias himself makes no claim to have been a hearer and eyewitness of the sacred apostles but rather indicates that he knew of their teaching at second hand.[36]

Papias compiled in five volumes *An Exegesis of the Dominical Logia*,[37] long since lost, except in so far as quotations from it are preserved in such writers as Irenaeus and Eusebius. It is probable, though not certain, that the *logia* of the title are oracles or sayings of Jesus. If the utterances of the ancient

---

represented at the end of a line by a stroke above the preceding vowel (ΑΠΕΓΡΑΨᾹ). (Lightfoot knew the Latin text of the prologue, though not its anti-Marcionite provenance, from a Vatican manuscript of the ninth century).

In the course of a discussion of this prologue in the correspondence columns of *The Times*, F. L. Cross wrote (13 February 1936): "My own reading of the prologue, if I may set it down dogmatically, is that in its original form it asserted that the fourth gospel was written by John the elder at the dictation of John the apostle when the latter had reached a very great age" (cf. A. Harnack, *Chronologie der altchristlichen Litteratur bis Eusebius*, i [Leipzig, 1897], p. 677). With Dr. Cross's suggestion we may compare the imaginary title-page composed for the Gospel by Dorothy L. Sayers: "*Memoirs of Jesus Christ. By John Bar-Zebedee*; edited by the Rev. John Elder, Vicar of St. Faith's, Ephesus" (*Unpopular Opinions* [London, 1946], p. 26).

35. Irenaeus, *Against Heresies* 5.33.4 (quoted by Eusebius, *Hist. Eccl.* 3.39.1).

36. *Hist. Eccl.* 3.39.2.

37. Eusebius, *Hist. Eccl.* 3.39.1.

prophets could be regarded as divine oracles,[38] the sayings of the Lord of the prophets were *a fortiori* entitled to be so described. Papias evidently preferred to make his compilation on the basis of oral tradition rather than by consulting written records, for in the introduction to his work he gives this account of his procedure:

> I will not hesitate to compile for you along with the interpretations all the things that I ever learned well from the elders and have kept well in mind, for I am convinced of their truth. Unlike most people, I did not find pleasure in those who have most to say but in those who teach the truth – in those who record, not other men's commandments, but the commandments given by the Lord to faith and proceeding from the truth itself. If ever any one came my way who had been in the company of the elders, I would enquire about the words of those elders. "What", I would ask, "did Andrew or Peter say, or Philip or Thomas or John or Matthew or any other of the Lord's disciples? And what do Aristion and John the elder, the Lord's disciples, say?" I did not think that what could be got from books helped me so much as what could be got from a living and abiding voice.[39]

This extract is preserved by Eusebius. If in places it is ambiguous, this may be due partly to our ignorance of its context (which has disappeared) and partly to a lack of precision in Papias's Greek style.[40]

---

38. For this use of λόγια cf. Acts 7:38; Romans 3:2; Heb. 5:12.
39. Quoted by Eusebius, *Hist. Eccl.* 3.39.3 f.
40. Here is one instance of ambiguity. From the words quoted Eusebius infers that, while Papias was not "a hearer and eyewitness of the holy apostles", he did actually hear Aristion and "the elder John"

By "elders" (*presbyteroi*) Papias probably meant, as
Irenaeus did later,[41] those early Christian leaders
who had known the immediate followers of Jesus –
leaders of the second Christian generation. This
usage may owe something to the Old Testament
statement that the Israelites, after their settlement in
Canaan, "served Yahweh all the days of Joshua [the
first post-settlement generation], and all the days of
the elders [LXX *presbyteroi*] who outlived Joshua [the
second generation]" (Josh. 24:31; Judg. 2:7).

We must not be side-tracked by other interpretative
problems in this passage but concentrate on the
twofold reference to John. When Papias met one of
the elders (or someone who had been in the
company of the elders) who had known the disciples
of the Lord he would ask what they heard from
those disciples. One of the disciples in question was
John, mentioned along with Andrew, Peter, Philip,[42]
Thomas and Matthew, all of whom we know to
have been members of the twelve; but there is a
further reference to John who is not only reckoned
among the Lord's disciples but is designated "the
elder". Are these two references to one and the
same John, or are they references to two distinct
Johns? We cannot be sure. If "elder" as applied to
him has the sense which it appears to have

(*Hist. Eccl.* 3.39. 2, 7). Eusebius knew the context of the words he
quoted, but we, without that knowledge, might readily infer that Papias
had only a hearsay acquaintance with what was said by Aristion and
"the elder John".

41. *Against Heresies* 5.5.1, etc.

42. It is a noteworthy coincidence that the sequence "Andrew, Peter,
Philip" is that in which the first disciples of Jesus are named in John
1:40–44. In this company Papias presumably refers to Philip the apostle,
of Bethsaida, not to Philip the evangelist, of Caesarea (even if the latter
did end his days in Hierapolis).

elsewhere in the passage, then the second reference would be to a John of the post-apostolic generation. Whereas Papias asked concerning one John, "What did he say?" he said concerning the other John, "What does he say?" And yet the second John, like the former, is called one of "the Lord's disciples". Was he the Nestor of the original disciples, surviving the others by a generation, and called "the elder" *par excellence* on that account? We do not overlook Aristion, who is mentioned in the second reference along with John as one of "the Lord's disciples"; but nothing more can be said of him as he appears to figure only in Papias who, according to Eusebius's interpretation of his words, "actually heard Aristion and the elder John . . . and gives their traditions in his writings".[43]

The earlier reference implies no association with the province of Asia for John any more than for the other members of the twelve whom it mentions; but such an association may be implied in the second reference: "What do Aristion and John the elder, the Lord's disciples, say?" The people whom Papias questioned were presumably some whom he met in his own province of Asia, and they would have more opportunity of knowing what Aristion and "John the elder" were currently saying if those two men were likewise accessible in the same province.

Eusebius understood Papias to refer to two distinct

43. *Hist. Eccl.* 3.39.7. B. H. Streeter made several suggestions about Aristion's contribution to early tradition (cf. *The Four Gospels* [London, 1924], pp. 344 ff.), the most venturesome being his "scientific" guess (as he hoped it might be called) that he was the author of 1 Peter (*The Primitive Church*, pp. 130 ff.).

Johns, and in this he may well have been right. But he had a special interest in distinguishing two Johns, since he did not appreciate the chiliasm of the Apocalypse and thought it inappropriate that so unacceptable a doctrine should be cloaked with the authority of the fourth evangelist, whom he identified unquestioningly with John the apostle. And yet the Apocalypse explicity claims to have been written by a man named John. Here in Papias, as Eusebius read him, was plain evidence of another, inferior, John, who might well be identified with the seer of Patmos, leaving the greater John untainted with chiliastic fantasy.

While the majority of recent and modern scholars, including such conservative nineteenth-century giants as S. P. Tregelles and J. B. Lightfoot,[44] would agree with Eusebius in understanding Papias as referring to two men called John, others have held that Papias made two references (albeit expressing himself clumsily) to one and the same John: among these may be mentioned F. W. Farrar, George Salmon, Theodor Zahn, John Chapman, Lawlor and Oulton, C. J. Cadoux and Stephen Smalley.[45] The question cannot be regarded as closed.

44. S. P. Tregelles, *The Historic Evidence of the Authorship and Transmission of the Books of the New Testament* (London. ²1881), p. 47; J. B. Lightfoot, *Essays on the Work Entitled "Supernatural Religion"*, p. 144 ("I cannot myself doubt that Eusebius was right in his interpretation").

45. F. W. Farrar, *The Early Days of Christianity* (London, 1882), pp. 618 ff.; G. Salmon, *Historical Introduction to the Study of the Books of the New Testament* (London, ⁴1889), pp. 287 ff.; T. Zahn, *Apostel und Apostelschüler in der Provinz Asien* (Leipzig, 1900), pp. 112 ff.; *Introduction to the New Testament*, E. T. (Edinburgh, 1909), ii. pp. 451 ff.; J. Chapman, *John the Presbyter and the Fourth Gospel* (Oxford, 1911), pp. 8 ff.; H. J. Lawlor and J. E. L. Oulton (tr.), *Eusebius: The Ecclesiastical History*, ii (London, 1928), p. 114; C. J. Cadoux, *Ancient Smyrna* (Oxford, 1938), pp. 316 ff.; S. S. Smalley, *John: Evangelist and Interpreter* (Exeter, 1978), pp. 73 f.

One further matter calls for attention before we leave Papias. One manuscript of the *Chronicle* of Georgios Hamartolos (who wrote about the year 840) states that Papias of Hierapolis, writing as an "eyewitness of John", recorded in his second book that John was " 'killed by Jews', thus fulfilling, along with his brother, Christ's prediction concerning them"[46] – a reference to Jesus' assurance to the two sons of Zebedee in Mark 10:38 that they would drink his cup and share his baptism. But this peculiar reading of one manuscript of Georgios's work may have been interpolated from a statement in an epitome of the fifth-century *Chronicle* of Philip of Sidé: "Papias in his second book says that John the divine and James his brother were killed by Jews".[47]

When the passage from the epitome of Philip's *Chronicle* was first published in 1888, it was inferred by some scholars that Papias must indubitably have said something to this effect.[48] But if he did, it is strange that Eusebius should have said nothing about it. If he had known of it, he might well have quoted it as conclusive evidence that Papias, as he

46. *Chronicle* 3.134.1. The manuscript is Codex Coislinianus 305, discovered in 1862.

47. Published by C. de Boor from the Bodleian MS. Baroccianus 142 in "Neue Fragmente des Papias, Hegesippus und Pierius", *Texte und Untersuchungen* 5.2 (1888), pp. 165 ff., especially p. 170. See J. A. Robinson, *Historical Character of St. John's Gospel* (London 1908), p. 66; J. Chapman, *John the Presbyter and the Fourth Gospel*, pp. 77 ff., 95 ff.; K. Lake and H. J. Cadbury, *The Acts of the Apostles = The Beginnings of Christianity*, iv (London, 1933), pp. 133 f.

48. Cf. E. Schwartz, "Ueber den Tod der Söhne Zebedaei", *Abhandlungen der kgl. Gesellschaft der Wissenschaften zu Göttingen*, phil.-hist. Kl., 7.5 (1907), pp. 266 ff.; "Noch einmal der Tod der Söhne Zebedaei", *ZNW* 11 (1910). pp. 89 ff.; J. Moffatt, *Introduction to the Literature of the New Testament* (Edinburgh, ³1918), pp. 603 ff.

put it, was a man of very small intelligence.[49] A critical examination of the statement attributed to Philip leads to the conclusion that it is a corruption of a passage which originally related the death of James the Just (not James the son of Zebedee), the brother of the Lord (not the brother of John).[50] The evidence on which the "critical myth" of John the apostle's early death rests is so flimsy that, as A. S. Peake put it, it "would have provoked derision if it had been adduced in favour of a conservative conclusion"[51] (which implies, no doubt rightly, that some people known to Peake were attracted by it because of its marked deviation from the preponderant voice of tradition).

6. *The witness of Dionysius*

Fifty years before Eusebius wrote, a more closely reasoned case for distinguishing the authors of the Fourth Gospel and the Apocalypse had been made by Dionysius, bishop of Alexandria. Dionysius presented stylistic and other critical arguments against the tradition that the John who names himself in the Apocalypse as its author was identical with the Fourth Evangelist, whom he believed to be John the apostle. He regarded the author of the Apocalypse as a "holy and divinely-inspired man" but

49. *Hist. Eccl.* 3.39.13; for the possibility that Eusebius might be quoting a self-depreciatory remark by Papias himself see J. R. Harris, *Testimonies*, i (Cambridge, 1916), pp. 119 f.

50. Cf. J. H. Bernard, *Studia Sacra* (London, 1917), pp. 260 ff., and *The Gospel according to St. John*, I.C.C. (Edinburgh, 1928), i, pp. xxxvii-xlv.

51. A. S. Peake, *Holborn Review* 19 (1928), p. 394, quoted by W. F. Howard, *The Fourth Gospel in Recent Criticism and Interpretation* (London, ⁴1955), p. 232; cf. Peake, *Critical Introduction to the New Testament* (London, 1909), pp. 142 ff.

thought that he was "a certain other [John] among those that were in Asia", adding that according to report there were "two tombs at Ephesus, each of which was said to be John's".[52] He does not mention Papias's twofold reference to John; perhaps he did not know it or perhaps he did not consider it to be relevant. Eusebius, however, found in the report of two tombs of John at Ephesus confirmation of the inference which he drew from Papias.

Of course the fact that two sites are pointed out as the tomb of a historical personage does not in itself imply that he or she must have been duplicated. We know that for a time in the third and fourth centuries two sites were venerated at Rome as the tomb of Peter and two as the tomb of Paul,[53] but no one has inferred from this that there were two Peters or two Pauls. The visitor to Jerusalem today may be shown two sites each claimed to be the place where Stephen the proto-martyr was stoned; but there was only one such Stephen. More importantly, he may be shown two rival sites for the crucifixion and burial of Jesus – one reflecting a tradition going back to the fourth (if not to the second) century, the other a tradition going back to the late nineteenth century – but no bizarre conclusions about dual identity have been drawn in this regard.

The two funerary traditions which Dionysius records appear to have survived at Ephesus into the present century. At least we are assured that at one time the former Greek inhabitants of Ayasoluk "used to worship, to decorate with wreaths and to light

---

52. Quoted by Eusebius, *Hist. Eccl.* 7.25.
53. See p. 47 with nn. 68, 69.

lamps before a simple arcosol-tomb cut into the rock, a little to the east of the ancient stadium [of Ephesus], as being the grave of St. John".[54] Robert Eisler, whom I have just quoted, provides a photograph of the rock-tomb in question;[55] lest it be thought that he is a dubious authority I should add that he is not the only writer of modern times to attest this tradition.[56]

Eisler thought there was a reference to this rock-tomb in one eleventh-century Greek manuscript of the *Acts of John*, which tells how, when John's friends came to remove his body from the grave (*orygma*) where it had been temporarily laid in order to deposit it "in the great church", they could not find it.[57] The reference to "the great church" implies that Justinian's basilica was now in existence, so that this passage forms no part of the original *Acts of John* (historically worthless as these *Acts* are). It may reflect the same local tradition as that which Dionysius mentions centuries before, but we have no means of knowing – any more than we have means of knowing if the burial-place venerated more

54. R. Eisler, *The Enigma of the Fourth Gospel*, p; 126;

55. *Ibid.*, Plate X, opposite p. 126 (reproduction of photograph by K. Lampakis in the photographic archives of the National Museum, Athens, No. 5982).

56. Eisler (*Enigma*, p. 127) expresses his indebtedness to Josef Keil, the excavator of Ephesus (see p. 123, n. 8 above), for drawing his attention to the photograph just mentioned and for expressing the view that the piety of local Christians attached itself to this rock-tomb in default of any other place to resort to. The tomb is marked GR (i.e. *Grab* "tomb") on A. Schindler and O. Benndorf's map of Ephesus (Abb. 2) in A. F. Pauly–G. Wissowa, *Realencyclopädie der klassischen Altertumswissenschaft* v, *s.v.* "Ephesos" (cols. 2773 ff.), immediately east of the stadium.

57. Eisler, *Enigma*, pp. 125 f. The manuscript (Paris gr. 1468) is listed as Q in E. Hennecke-W. Schneemelcher - R. McL. Wilson, *New Testament Apocrypha*, ii (London, 1965), pp. 195 ff.

recently in the vicinity of the stadium attests the continuity of that tradition.

7. *The Johannine circle*

From the time of Dionysius of Alexandria, then, there have been students who, on stylistic or other grounds, have distinguished the John who wrote the Apocalypse from the Fourth Evangelist.[58] They have not all, like Dionysius himself and Eusebius, identified the Evangelist with John the son of Zebedee and the seer of Patmos with some other John. Justin Martyr, writing about the middle of the second century, identified the seer of Patmos with the apostle,[59] and some scholars of more recent time have found it more probable that the apostle was the author of the Apocalypse than that he composed the Fourth Gospel. One who was so little a traditionalist as C. J. Cadoux found the evidence leading "to the conclusion that the Apostle John did survive to a great age in Ephesos, and was himself the writer of the 'Apocalypse' ".[60] He was, on the other hand, far from admitting the apostolic authorship of the Fourth Gospel.

But it was generally accepted that the three

58. In earlier days they were in the minority. Towards the end of the second century the anti-Marcionite prologue to Luke ends with the words: "And later John the apostle, one of the twelve, wrote the Apocalypse on the island of Patmos and after that the Gospel". C. H. Dodd dismisses the idea that the same person could have been responsible for both works with the Horatian tag: *credat Judaeus Apella, non ego!* (*The Interpretation of the Fourth Gospel* [Cambridge, 1953], p. 215, n. 3).

59. *Dialogue with Trypho* 81.4. Justin seems to have known the Fourth Gospel, but gives no hint of its authorship.

60. *Ancient Smyrna*, p. 317.

Epistles of John (and especially the first) came from the same author as the Fourth Gospel. When in 1911 Dom John Chapman wrote that "no sane critic will deny that the Gospel and the first Epistle are from the same pen",[61] he would have commanded the assent of the great majority of British scholars. Presumably, he excluded from the category of "sane scholar" some writers (mainly German) who had discerned diverse authors for the two documents. But in 1936 one whom none would refuse to call a sane scholar, C. H. Dodd, delivered a lecture on "The First Epistle of John and the Fourth Gospel", and argued on linguistic and theological grounds that the author of the epistle was not the Evangelist himself but one of his disciples.[62] He amplified his argument in his Moffatt Commentary on the Epistles of John, which was published in 1946.[63] In the following year another eminent Johannine scholar of the same generation, W. F. Howard, subjected Dodd's argument to a careful examination and concluded that "there is so much that is common to Gospel and Epistle, both in language and in thought, that presumptive evidence favours the substantial unity of authorship".[64]

61. *John the Presbyter and the Fourth Gospel*, p. 72. A list of earlier writers who had denied identity of authorship for the two documents will be found in Moffatt, *Introduction*[3], pp. 589 f.

62. "The First Epistle of John and the Fourth Gospel", *BJRL* 21 (1937), pp. 129–156.

63. *The Johannine Epistles* (London, 1946), pp. xlvii ff.

64. "The Common Authorship of the Johannine Gospel and Epistles", *JTS* 48 (1947), pp. 12–25, reprinted in *The Fourth Gospel in Recent Criticism and Interpretation*[4], pp. 282 ff. Dr. Howard thought that the Epistles were written by the evangelist towards the end of his life, while the Fourth Gospel "represents his meditations and teaching over a number of years and was *published* after his death" (*Christianity according to St. John* [London, 1943], p. 18, n. 2). Cf. T. W. Manson's argument that, if we

It is not our present purpose to investigate the literary relationships of the Johannine documents of the New Testament. But these documents themselves point to the existence of what may be called a "Johannine circle".[65] We may think of the anonymous writers of the note at the end of the Fourth Gospel who ascribe its authorship to the beloved disciple and add "we know that his witness is true" (John 21:24). We may think of the recipients of 1 John, whom the writer calls his "little children", of the elect ladies and their children mentioned in 2 John, and of Gaius, Demetrius and other friends who receive honourable mention in 3 John. The author of 2 and 3 John calls himself "the elder" – the designation by which he was presumably known to those friends of his. The author of 1 John gives himself no designation at all, but since he calls his readers his "little children" they too may well have called him "the elder", meaning simply (and affectionately) "the old man". The coincidence between

are to "examine the Johannine theology [i.e. the theology of the Fourth Evangelist] in its relatively pure state", then "the proper method is to begin with the [first] Epistle and there find what are the leading theological ideas of the author" (*On Paul and John* [London, 1963], pp. 87 f.).

65. W. F. Howard (*Christianity according to St. John*, p. 15) quotes with approval a "significant remark" of J. Weiss to the effect that all five Johannine writings "came from the same circle, in the same region of the Church, about the same time" (*Die Offenbarung des Johannes* [Göttingen, 1904], pp. 162 ff.) J. B. Lightfoot had earlier spoken of "the school of St. John" (i.e. the apostle) in proconsular Asia, which in the first generation included John the elder, in the second Papias and Polycarp, in the third Melito of Sardis and Apollinaris of Hierapolis, and in the fourth Polycrates of Ephesus; he discerned this ongoing "school" in the repeated references by Irenaeus (*Against Heresies* 2.22.5; 3.3.4, etc.) to "the elders who in Asia associated with John the disciple of the Lord", "the church in Ephesus . . . the true witness of the apostolic tradition" and so forth (*Essays on the Work Entitled "Supernatural Religion"*. pp. 217 ff.; cf. his *Biblical Essays* [London. 1893], pp. 51 ff.).

this designation in the Johannine letters and Papias's mention of "the elder John" may be a *mere* coincidence, but it may be more.

In the mid-seventies two important monographs appeared on the Johannine circle. One, by Oscar Cullmann, was devoted to "the origin, character and setting of the 'Johannine circle', which stands behind the [Fourth] Gospel and continues its theological concern. The existence of this circle", he adds, "can hardly be challenged."[66]

The other, by R. A. Culpepper, goes farther than envisaging a vague "circle" and argues that there was a clearly defined Johannine "school", which reproduced the constant features found in other schools of Greek and Jewish antiquity – the philosophical schools of the Greeks and the rabbinical schools of the Jews (not excluding the "school" to which the disciples of Jesus belonged).[67]

The Johannine circle or school had its leaders, among whom the author(s) of the Johannine documents may be discerned. One conjecture regarding their identity and relationship is put forward tentatively by C. K. Barrett: "that the evangelist, the author – or authors . . .– of the epistles, and the final editor of Revelation were all pupils of the original apocalyptist. They developed his work on similar lines, but it was the evangelist who saw

66. O. Cullmann, *The Johannine Circle*, E. T. (London, 1976), p. ix.
67. R. A. Culpepper, *The Johannine School: An Evaluation of the Johannine-School Hypothesis based on an Investigation of the Nature of Ancient Schools* (Missoula, Montana, 1975). See also D. M. Smith, "Johannine Christianity: Some Reflections on its Character and Delineation", NTS 21 (1974–75), pp. 222–248; E. S. Fiorenza, "The Quest for the Johannine School: The Apocalypse and the Fourth Gospel", NTS 23 (1976–77), pp. 402–427. R. E. Brown has now produced a major study entitled *The Community of the Beloved Disciple* (New York/London, 1979).

most clearly how eschatological Christian theology could be re-expressed in the language of Hellenistic thought, and indeed saw this so clearly as to be far ahead of his time."[68]

Professor Barrett recognizes a relationship between the Apocalypse and the Fourth Gospel; indeed, in spite of their obvious differences, the two documents share an impressive number of common features and certainly come from the same circle. If the apocalyptist was John the son of Zebedee (which is not at all improbable), he could be regarded as the founder of the circle, which would then be most fittingly called the Johannine circle. If Papias's "John the elder" is a distinct person from the son of Zebedee, then he may be regarded as a distinguished member of the circle, and possibly as the one who succeeded to its leadership when the apostle died.[69]

In an article published in 1930,[70] Alphonse Mingana mentioned that some Peshitta manuscripts contain a treatise ascribed to Eusebius, which gives a short account of each of the twelve apostles and seventy disciples (though Eusebius says that "no list of the Seventy is anywhere extant").[71] The section on John, translated from Mingana's Syriac quotation, is as follows:

68. *The Gospel according to St. John* (London, [2] 1978), p. 62; cf. pp. 133 f. Forty years earlier R. H. Charles had expressed the view that "the Evangelist was apparently at one time a disciple of the Seer, or they were members of the same religious circle in Ephesus" (*The Revelation of St. John*, I.C.C. [Edinburgh, 1920], i. p. xxxiii).
69. In the fourth-century *Apostolic Constitutions* a list of bishops allegedly appointed in various churches by apostles includes "in Ephesus, . . . John appointed by me, John" (7.46). The historical value of the list is *nil*, except that the *names* are not inventions (but the second John probably represents an inference from Eusebius).
70. "The Authorship of the Fourth Gospel", *BJRL* 14 (1930), pp. 333 ff.
71. *Hist. Eccl.*, 1.12.1.

John the Evangelist was also from Bethsaida. He was
of the tribe of Zebulun. He preached in Asia at first,
and afterwards was banished by Tiberius Caesar to the
isle of Patmos. Then he went to Ephesus and built up
the church in it. Three of his disciples went thither
with him, and there he died and was buried. [These
three were] Ignatius, who was afterwards bishop in
Antioch and was thrown to the beasts at Rome;
Polycarp, who was afterwards bishop of Smyrna and
was crowned [as a martyr] in the fire; John, to whom
he committed the priesthood and the episcopal see
after him. He then [the Evangelist], having lived a long
time, died and was buried in Ephesus, in which he
had been bishop. He was buried by his disciple John,
who was bishop in Ephesus [after him]; and their two
graves are in Ephesus – one concealed, namely the
Evangelist's; the other being that of John his disciple,
who wrote the Revelations (*gelyane*), for he said that he
heard all that he wrote from the mouth of the
Evangelist.

Though not the work of Eusebius, this section is
certainly based on him and on his report of
Dionysius of Alexandria's views of the Apocalypse.
But, unlike Dionysius and Eusebius, it does not
make the second John the author of the Apocalypse,
but simply the amanuensis of the apostle, who was
the real author – unless indeed, as some think, the
plural "Revelations" refers not to the Apocalypse but
to the Gospel, in which case an early precedent
would be provided for those writers of our day
who, believing in a second John at Ephesus, regard
him as the apostle's amanuensis (or more than
amanuensis) in the writing of the Gospel. The
statement that John was banished to Patmos by

Tiberius must be set down as a sheer blunder, warning us not to treat the passage too seriously.

This Syriac treatise hardly provides *independent* evidence for the Ephesian residence and episcopate of a second John. But Mingana gave further interesting information. Peshitta manuscripts regularly have this colophon after the Fourth Gospel: "Here ends the Gospel of John who spoke in Greek at Ephesus." But one manuscript (Mingana Syriac 540) has the unique colophon: "Here ends the writing of the holy Gospel – the preaching of John who spoke in Greek in *Bithynia*"; and also the unique prefatory note: "The holy Gospel of our Lord Jesus Christ – the preaching of John the younger" (*Yuḥanan naʿarā'*). The manuscript is dated 1749, but was copied from one dated by Mingana a thousand years earlier. Mingana very cautiously suggested the inference that this "younger John" was the disciple of the apostle mentioned in the treatise just referred to; but if so, the apostle must have been (in relation to him, at least), the *elder* John. The reference to Bithynia in the colophon may simply be a mistake arising out of ignorance. W. F. Howard summed up Mingana's discovery with wise caution: "Interesting as this is, we can hardly treat it as other than a bit of irresponsible guesswork by some scribe of a late date in the history of the transcription of the Gospel".[72] It belongs to the same category as the notes on author, amanuensis, place of writing, etc. appended to various New Testament epistles, which the Authorized Version has taken over from the *Textus Receptus*.

72. W. F. Howard, "St. John: The Story of the Book", in *The Story of the Bible* (Amalgamated Press, 1938), p. 1233.

The identity of John the apocalyptist with the son of Zebedee, I said, is not at all improbable. But this would not be universally conceded. For one thing, the apocalyptist claims to be a prophet, not an apostle;[73] for another, if Tertullian is using accurate legal terminology when he describes John as *in insulam relegatus*,[74] then, it is argued, John must have belonged to the *honestiores*, the more reputable classes of society, whether Roman or Jewish.[75] Victorinus of Pettau (died 303), the earliest Latin commentator on the Apocalypse, says that John was sentenced to penal servitude in the mines or quarries (*in metallo*) of Patmos,[76] but there is no evidence that there were such installations on Patmos or that criminals were sent there for hard labour.[77] J. N. Sanders, who inferred from Tertullian's reference that John of Patmos belonged to the upper classes of Jewish society, argued further that if John's *relegatio* was imposed for his Christian activity – "for the word of God and the testimony of Jesus", as he says himself (Rev. 1:9) – it must have been before such activity became a capital offence, that is, before A.D. 64/65; and that he may have been the "other

73. "He never makes any claim to apostleship: . . . he distinctly claims to be a prophet" (R. H. Charles, *The Revelation of St. John*, I.C.C., i, p. xliii).

74. Tertullian, *De praescriptione haereticorum*, 36.

75. Cf. J. N. Sanders, "St. John on Patmos", *NTS* 9 (1962–3), pp. 75–85 (especially p. 76).

76. Victorinus, *In Apocalypsim* (on Rev. 10:11), ed. J. Haussleiter, *CSEL* 49 (Vindobonae, 1916), p. 92.

77. G. B. Caird (*The Revelation of St. John the Divine* [London, 1966], p. 21 with n. 2) shows how this idea, first put out as a conjecture, has been taken over by one writer from another "as though it were a well attested fact"; he adds that Pliny the elder, who is repeatedly invoked as an authority for this alleged fact, says nothing more about Patmos than that it is thirty miles round (*Nat. Hist.* 4.69).

disciple" of John 18: 15 f. who was "known", and possibly related, to the high priest.[78] Sanders went farther along the road of speculation than this, but unless speculation is held on a tight rein it very quickly loses all credibility; so we may leave it at that.

An apostle, let it be said, is not debarred from exercising the gift of prophecy by the fact of his being an apostle, and since the Apocalypse is expressly presented as a prophecy the author would naturally introduce himself as a prophet rather than as an apostle. And, even if Tertullian meant *relegatio* in its precise legal sense, we do not know if he had any firm evidence that this was in fact the nature of John's banishment to Patmos.

Whoever the seer of Patmos was, he was deemed to be a suitable messenger to convey the apocalyptic warnings and encouragements to the churches of Ephesus and other Asian cities, and the contents of the seven letters addressed to those churches indicate that he was fairly well acquainted with their local circumstances.

The Ephesian contacts of the Fourth Gospel and the Johannine epistles are not so explicit. Some scholars in more recent times have tried to link these documents rather with Syrian Antioch,[79] or even with Egyptian Alexandria.[80] Their internal evi-

---

78. "St. John on Patmos", p. 85: "John of Ephesus, the seer and exile of Patmos, was a Sadducean aristocrat, a Jerusalem disciple of Jesus, and last survivor of the eye-witness of the incarnate Logos, but not the son of Zebedee." Cf. p. 127, n. 19.

79. Cf. C. F. Burney, *The Aramaic Origin of the Fourth Gospel* (Oxford, 1922), pp. 129 ff., 171.

80. Cf. K. and S. Lake, *Introduction to the New Testament* (London, 1938), p. 53 f.; J. N. Sanders, *The Fourth Gospel in the Early Church*

dence has little to say in this regard. The main argument for a link with Syrian Antioch is based on the affinities with Johannine thought discerned in the letters of Ignatius, who was bishop of the church in that city. Professor Cullmann mentions also the links between the Fourth Gospel and the *Odes of Solomon*, which he believes "come from this area". Syria, then, is one of two areas to which he assigns "a great degree of probability" as the place of origin of the Fourth Gospel and the related documents, adding (remarkably enough) Transjordan as "the other possibility which can be supported with strong (perhaps even stronger) arguments".[81] (This inclination towards Transjordan is bound up with his long-standing interest in the Pseudo-Clementines and the origins of Jewish Christianity.)[82] The Ephesian provenance he finds "much less well founded", although he agrees that even apart from the voice of tradition there are points which tell in its favour. He notes among these "the presence in Asia Minor of the heresies attacked in the Gospel of John, and in particular of a group of disciples of John [the Baptist]".[83]

Neither in Syria nor anywhere else, however, do

(Cambridge, 1943), pp. 85 ff. (Sanders later changed his mind and accepted Ephesus as the place where the Gospel was written; see J. N. Sanders and B. A. Mastin, *The Gospel according to St. John* [London, 1968], p. 51); J. L. Martyn, *History and Theology in the Fourth Gospel* (New York, 1968), p. 58, n. 94; W. H. Brownlee, "Whence the Gospel according to John?" in *John and Qumran* ed. J. H. Charlesworth (London, 1972), pp. 189–191.

81. O. Cullmann, *The Johannine Circle*, pp. 98 f.

82. Cf. O. Cullmann, *Le problème littéraire et historique du roman pseudoclémentin* (Paris, 1930). See p. 118, n. 59.

83. *The Johannine Circle*, p. 99. If the "group of disciples of John" is identified with the twelve disciples of Acts 19:1–7, the identification is precarious; see p. 70.

we find the weight of tradition and external testimony that links the Johannine literature and its author or authors with Ephesus. In the absence of any tradition or substantial evidence to the contrary, the Ephesian link holds the field.

8. Conclusion

The traditional figure of St. John the divine, the "holy theologian" whose name is commemorated by the hill and basilica of Ayasoluk, may be a composite figure, in whom John the apostle and John the elder have been fused. But they would not have been fused so long as people remained alive who remembered them both. The idea that any one who remembered them both would have confounded the one with the other is improbable in the extreme. "No phenomenon", said I. T. Beckwith, "is better attested than trustworthy recollections of the identity of persons seen and heard half a century before".[84] Irenaeus, he adds, nowhere undertakes to *prove* that John the apostle lived in Asia: he refers to his residence incidentally, as something which was common knowledge. Those who knew John the apostle and John the elder would have no difficulty in distinguishing them, especially if (as is probable) the elder survived the apostle.

To conclude: the basilica of St. John commemorates a Christian tradition going back, as surely as do the Roman basilicas of St. Peter and St. Paul, to the mid-second century, and probably earlier still. Even

84. I. T. Beckwith, *The Apocalypse of John* (London, 1919), p. 376. Beckwith's discussion of "The Two Johns of the Asian Church" (pp. 362–393) is a model of sober and lucid inquiry.

in its ruined state it bears silent witness to those "great luminaries" who fell asleep in proconsular Asia, among whom "John the disciple of the Lord" (with his school or circle) occupies a pre-eminent place.

INDEX